Growing Together

THE **FAMILY** DEVOTIONAL

Growing Together

THE **FAMILY** DEVOTIONAL

CWR

STEVE AND BEKAH LEGG

Contents

Introduction

Choices.

We face choices every day – from what to wear and what to eat, to what to do with our free time. We can choose whether to be nice and share; how helpful we're going to be and how kind; whether to listen to other people or not.

Some choices are more important than others, and as we get older it can feel like they get bigger and bigger. Suddenly, choices include which school to go to, which subjects to study and then what job to have.

Our choices matter. Every little one has a consequence, and we want to help you think about what you choose to do with the time and gifts that you have.

How do you usually enjoy spending your time? Maybe you sit and watch TV, play with the dog, read a book or chat with your friends. One of the reasons why we wrote this book is because we think it's important to spend some time together as a family, talking about things that really matter.

It's so easy nowadays to love each other but forget to spend good time together. But choosing to put your gadgets down for a while to really enjoy each other's company is so worth it, and we hope this book will help you have some good conversations – whether that's at bedtime, or over a meal, or at another point in the day. It's great to ask questions and find out what you all think about different things. What do you have in common? What differences do you have?

We also know it's worth choosing to spend some time with God, getting to know Him together. It can be even easier to forget to spend time with Him, but we think it's the most important thing anyone can do. So, we've chosen some stories from the Bible that will help you get to know Him a bit better.

You'll read about people like Joshua, Deborah and Elijah, who all knew God and did some amazing things for Him. They had to make some really big choices, and they didn't always get it right. We'll also find out about some of the people that met Jesus face-to-face on earth and how they chose to respond to Him when He was right in front of them. Often, they didn't do what you might expect – in fact, some of them made choices that seem downright crazy!

By looking at some of these stories, you'll get to see just how amazing God is. You'll see Him make huge promises that He always keeps; stick by people even when they make mistakes; protect people when they are in terrible danger; and love people even when they choose to turn away from Him. He's an awesome God.

One of the biggest choices any of us ever make is how to respond to Jesus ourselves. Jesus loves you and wants you to know Him and spend time with Him. Our hope is that this book will help you to do just that.

We pray that God will bless the choice you've already made to open this book up for the first time. Our prayer for you over the next 12 weeks is that, as a family, you will grow closer together, discover new things about each other as you meet with Jesus, and deepen your relationship with God. We pray you'll learn to hear God speak to you through the pages of the Bible and that you'll know His presence with you through any tough choices and challenges you face.

As you journey through these 12 weeks, we hope you enjoy it so much that you'll want to continue spending time together with God, and that this is part of a whole lifetime of following wherever He leads you.

Bekah

Operation: explore

Numbers 13:1–2,17–20

'The LORD said to Moses, "Choose one of the leaders from each of the twelve tribes and send them as spies to explore the land of Canaan, which I am giving to the Israelites...

When Moses sent them out, he said to them, "Go north from here into the southern part of the land of Canaan and then on into the hill country. Find out what kind of country it is, how many people live there, and how strong they are. Find out whether the land is good or bad and whether the people live in open towns or in fortified cities. Find out whether the soil is fertile and whether the land is wooded. And be sure to bring back some of the fruit that grows there."'

Something to think about

The people of God, the Israelites, were about to get a new home. God had rescued them from Egypt, where they'd lived as slaves, and since then they'd been wandering for years in the wilderness and living in tents. Finally, God was ready to give them a land of their own. He asked Moses, their leader, to send 12 other leaders to check out the land. It was an awesome privilege: these men would be the first to see their new home. But it was a responsibility too: they needed to tell everyone else what to expect – people couldn't check it out for themselves on the internet!

Bekah says...

God wants everyone in the world to know Him and be part of His Kingdom, and if you're reading this, it means you've been given the opportunity to play a part in that happening. It's both an awesome privilege and a responsibility to tell others about what it's like to be friends with Jesus.

Steve's amazing fact

Ernest Shackleton was an amazing British explorer who led three expeditions to the Antarctic. He said, 'I had a dream when I was 22 that someday I would go to the region of ice and snow and go on and on till I came to one of the poles of the earth.' He did just that.

Something to talk about

· When have you been the first to get to do something exciting?
· How did that make you feel?

Pray

Father God, thank You for inviting me to get to know You. Help me to explore the world with You by my side and to tell other people about what it's like to live with You. Amen.

Giants!

Numbers 13:25–28,31–33

'After exploring the land for forty days, the spies returned...
They said to Moses, "We explored the land and found it
to be rich and fertile; and here is some of its fruit. But
the people who live there are powerful, and their cities
are very large and well fortified. Even worse, we saw the
descendants of the giants there."...

"No, we are not strong enough to attack them; the people
there are more powerful than we are." So they spread
a false report among the Israelites about the land they
had explored. They said, "That land doesn't even produce
enough to feed the people who live there. Everyone
we saw was very tall, and we even saw giants there, the
descendants of Anak. We felt as small as grasshoppers, and
that is how we must have looked to them."'

Something to think about

The spies came back, full of news, but they didn't tell their
friends the good things they'd seen – only the bad. They
tried to persuade everyone not to bother following God
into this new land.

Sometimes it can be easy to focus on the things that scare
us or the things we can't do, forgetting the good things and

what we *can* do. When we get all caught up in worries and fear, just like these spies from Israel, we can miss out on some awesome stuff! It's really important that we look at the good as well as the bad when we're making big decisions or trying something new.

Bekah says...

One of our girls really struggles with feeling anxious, especially when it comes to tests and exams. The worries can take over her mind and make her think she can't do it. But we know she can! We have to remind her of the good stuff: that tests aren't the end of the world, that she has worked very hard and will be fine, and that God is always with her. We're really proud of how she fights her fears and has a go anyway.

Something to talk about

· Have you ever missed out on something because you were scared?
· What helps you to be brave?

Pray

Dear God, thank You for always being with us and for giving us courage to face our fears. Amen.

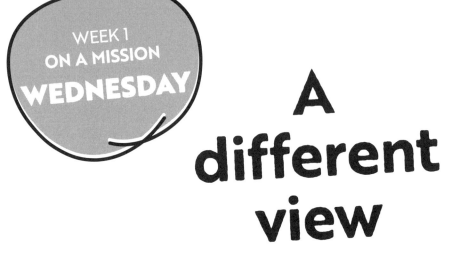

A different view

Numbers 14:6–9

'And Joshua son of Nun and Caleb son of Jephunneh, two of the spies, tore their clothes in sorrow and said to the people, "The land we explored is an excellent land. If the LORD is pleased with us, he will take us there and give us that rich and fertile land. Do not rebel against the LORD and don't be afraid of the people who live there. We will conquer them easily. The LORD is with us and has defeated the gods who protected them; so don't be afraid."'

Something to think about

Joshua and Caleb were different to the other spies. They'd all been to the same place, tasted the same food and seen the same giant people, but this pair saw it differently. The other spies had looked with fear at what they found, but Joshua and Caleb remembered who their God was and looked at the new land with that knowledge and confidence. It changed everything. Yes, there were scary people there, but they weren't bigger than God.

These two knew how awesome their God was and that with Him they could do anything. God had promised to give the land to His people, the Israelites, and Joshua and Caleb trusted Him to do it. We can trust God in the same way too: if He makes us a promise, He keeps it, no matter how impossible it seems.

Steve says...

A giant (a person with a condition called gigantism) is generally considered to be anyone over 7 feet tall. At 6'3" myself, I'm way off that. The tallest man recorded in history was Robert Wadlow from the USA. When last measured in 1940, he was found to be 8'11.1" tall. That is seriously big.

Something to talk about

· What promises has God made to you?
· What helps you to trust Him?

Pray

Father God, thank You for Your promise to love us and to give us hope and a future. Help us to look at the world around us, remembering that You are always with us and knowing that we have You on our side. Amen.

Not enough

Numbers 14:10–11,20–23

'The whole community was threatening to stone them to death, but suddenly the people saw the dazzling light of the LORD's presence appear over the tent.

The LORD said to Moses, "How much longer will these people reject me? How much longer will they refuse to trust in me, even though I have performed so many miracles among them?"...

"I will forgive them, as you have asked. But I promise that as surely as I live and as surely as my presence fills the earth, none of these people will live to enter that land. They have seen the dazzling light of my presence and the miracles that I performed in Egypt and in the wilderness, but they have tried my patience over and over again and have refused to obey me. They will never enter the land which I promised to their ancestors."'

Something to think about

Joshua and Caleb had spoken the truth to God's people, but no one was interested. They had heard about the giants and didn't trust God to look after them. God even showed up in the most amazing way so that everyone could see, and still His people didn't believe He would look after them. Because of that, they missed out on everything God promised their grandparents; none of them would see the Promised Land. Only their children would.

Bekah says...

It always surprises me that people could see such amazing miracles and still not trust God. These people had seen the ten plagues, escaped from Egypt, walked through the Red Sea, been fed miraculously in the desert, and they still didn't trust God.

It's possible to see God do incredible things and still not really get who He is. I've heard people say, 'If God would just do something amazing for me, then I'd follow Him.' But I'm not sure they would. Following God is a decision to make because you choose to believe He's good, not because He's proved Himself to you in the way you think He should.

Something to talk about

· Why did you choose to follow Jesus?
· Have you ever seen Him do something amazing in your life?

Pray

Dear God, I choose to follow You on the good days and the bad, and to trust that You will keep me safe. Amen.

Passing the baton

Deuteronomy 31:7; Joshua 1:7–9

'Then Moses called Joshua and said to him in the presence of all the people of Israel, "Be determined and confident; you are the one who will lead these people to occupy the land that the LORD promised to their ancestors.'

'Just be determined, be confident; and make sure that you obey the whole Law that my servant Moses gave you. Do not neglect any part of it and you will succeed wherever you go. Be sure that the book of the Law is always read in your worship. Study it day and night, and make sure that you obey everything written in it. Then you will be prosperous and successful. Remember that I have commanded you to be determined and confident! Do not be afraid or discouraged, for I, the LORD your God, am with you wherever you go."'

Something to think about

God's people lived in the desert for years before it was finally time to enter their new country. Now, Moses knew it was also time to let someone else become the leader, and that Joshua, who had already shown how much he trusted God, was the right person for the job. Moses had confidence in Joshua and so did God. God told Joshua to remember that He would always be with him, wherever he went. And He told him one other really important thing too: read the book of the Law (to us, that's the Bible) all the time. God had given His people a way of remembering Him and His ways, and He's given it to us too. It matters that we read it often.

Steve's amazing fact

Running a relay race means getting a lot of things right. You need just the right runners for the different positions – for example, someone with a good start to go first and someone who is good at running in a straight line to go second. You also have to pass the baton at just the right time in just the right place, otherwise the whole team is disqualified.

Something to talk about

· How easy do you find reading the Bible?
· What helps you to understand it and know what it means?

Pray

Father God, thank You for having confidence in us to carry out Your plan. Help us to read the Bible so we can get to know You and Your plans better. Amen.

Crossing the Jordan

Joshua 3:9–13,15–17

'Then Joshua said to the people, "Come here and listen to what the LORD your God has to say. As you advance, he will surely drive out the Canaanites, the Hittites, the Hivites, the Perizzites, the Girgashites, the Amorites, and the Jebusites. You will know that the living God is among you when the Covenant Box of the Lord of all the earth crosses the Jordan ahead of you... When the priests who carry the Covenant Box of the LORD of all the earth put their feet in the water, the Jordan will stop flowing, and the water coming downstream will pile up in one place."...

As soon as the priests stepped into the river, the water stopped flowing and piled up, far upstream at Adam, the city beside Zarethan. The flow downstream to the Dead Sea was completely cut off, and the people were able to cross over near Jericho. While the people walked across on dry ground, the priests carrying the LORD's Covenant Box stood on dry ground in the middle of the Jordan until all the people had crossed over.'

Something to think about

It was time. The moment had come for the Israelites to follow God into the new land, and God gave them a new promise – that He was stronger than the scary people who already lived there and that He would make a place for His people there. Then He went on to do an amazing miracle – one a bit like He had done when He rescued the Israelites' grandparents from Egypt, making a way for them through the Red Sea. It would have been the most awesome reminder of how mighty God was.

Something to talk about
· Have you ever seen God do something amazing that helped you know how big and strong He is?
· How could you make sure you remember it?

Pray
God, thank You for the amazing things You have done in my life. Please help me not to forget them. Amen.

Something for the weekend
The Israelites went on to set up a memorial to remember what God did for them the day they crossed the river without getting wet! Why not create a memorial of a day when God did something amazing for you? You might like to frame a photo, write a memory down or even decorate and keep your own special rock.

Danger in Jericho

Joshua 2:1–6

'Then Joshua sent two spies from the camp at Acacia with orders to go and secretly explore the land of Canaan, especially the city of Jericho. When they came to the city, they went to spend the night in the house of... Rahab. The king of Jericho heard that some Israelites had come that night to spy out the country, so he sent word to Rahab: "The men in your house have come to spy out the whole country! Bring them out!"

"Some men did come to my house," she answered, "but I don't know where they were from. They left at sunset... before the city gate was closed. I didn't find out where they were going, but if you start after them quickly, you can catch them." (Now Rahab had taken the two spies up on the roof and hidden them under some stalks of flax that she had put there.)'

Something to think about

Jericho was a strong city that no one dared to attack, but it lay right in the heart of the land God had promised His people and contained a really important source of water. Joshua sent some spies to check the city out, but the king of Jericho found out, which meant they were in real danger. Rahab was not an important or respected woman to those around her, but she protected these spies even though they were strangers. That was a really brave thing for her to do.

Bekah says...

I work with a charity that has brought refugee families into the UK and given them somewhere safe to live and the chance to start a new life. I didn't know the families who came, but I know that if I was in danger, I'd hope someone would help me.

Steve's amazing fact

In 1938, Jewish people in Europe were under threat from the Nazis. Nicholas Winton, a young man working in London, was horrified by what was happening. He travelled to Prague and came up with a plan that rescued and saved the lives of hundreds of children, just before the start of the Second World War.

Something to talk about

· When have you gone out of your way to care for someone?
· What made you do it?

Pray

Dear Lord Jesus, You came to this world to save me even before I was born. Help me to look out for other people the same way You look out for me. Amen.

God is famous

Joshua 2:8–14

'Before the spies settled down for the night, Rahab went up on the roof and said to them, "I know that the LORD has given you this land. Everyone in the country is terrified of you. We have heard how the LORD dried up the Red Sea in front of you when you were leaving Egypt... The LORD your God is God in heaven above and here on earth. Now swear by him that you will treat my family as kindly as I have treated you, and give me some sign that I can trust you. Promise me that you will save my father and mother, my brothers and sisters, and all their families! Don't let us be killed!"

The men said to her, "May God take our lives if we don't do as we say! If you do not tell anyone what we have been doing, we promise you that when the LORD gives us this land, we will treat you well."'

Something to think about

Rahab had heard all about the spies' God. She'd heard the stories – their God was famous. But most importantly, she'd heard the stories and realised what they meant – their God was the one true God. That's why she'd chosen to help these spies. She recognised who God was, and now she wanted to know if His people would look after her too.

The spies now had a really important decision to make,

because they were God's representatives to this lady. What they did next would have a huge impact on Rahab and her family. Thankfully, they chose to show God's love and promised to look after them all.

Bekah says...

It's good for us to remember that we're God's representatives on earth too. It's a big challenge to represent Him well.

Steve's amazing fact

In a recent YouGov poll, Simon Cowell proved more popular in the UK than the Queen, David Beckham and Kim Kardashian. Also up there in the top five most famous people in the UK were Madonna, Leonardo DiCaprio, Prince Harry and Gordon Ramsay.

Something to talk about

- When have you shown God's love to people who don't know Him?
- Do you have a situation right now in which you can represent God well?

Pray

Father God, help me to be just like You in every situation I find myself in – at school, at work and at home. Amen.

Promise makers

Joshua 2:15–18,21–23

'Rahab lived in a house built into the city wall, so she let the men down from the window by a rope. "Go into the hill country," she said, "or the king's men will find you. Hide there for three days until they come back. After that, you can go on your way."

The men said to her, "We will keep the promise that you have made us give... When we invade your land, tie this red cord to the window you let us down from. Get your father and mother, your brothers, and all your father's family together in your house."...

When they had gone, she tied the red cord to the window.

The spies went into the hills and hid. The king's men looked for them all over the countryside for three days, but they did not find them, so they returned to Jericho. Then the two spies... went back to Joshua. They told him everything that had happened'

Something to think about

The spies were more than just good talkers – they kept their promises. They came up with a plan for Rahab to be saved, and the first thing they did when they got back was tell their leader Joshua all about it. It would have been very easy for them to make their promise to Rahab so that she would protect them, and then choose not to follow through with it once they were out of danger. They could have also easily forgotten about it. But they didn't. They stuck to it.

Bekah says...

Keeping our promises is much easier if we are careful to only promise things we can actually do. Try not to promise things unless you are really sure they're possible and you want to follow through with them.

Steve says...

We can all struggle to keep our promises. For politicians, it matters even more that they keep to what they have said. One prime minister once said: 'It is easy to make promises – it is hard work to keep them.'

Something to talk about

· Have you ever made a promise you couldn't keep?
· How did that make you feel?

Pray

Father God, thank You for always keeping Your promises. Help me to be like You and to be someone people can trust. Amen.

A crazy plan

Joshua 6:1–7

'The gates of Jericho were kept shut and guarded to keep the Israelites out... The LORD said to Joshua, "I am putting into your hands Jericho, with its king and all its brave soldiers. You and your soldiers are to march around the city once a day for six days. Seven priests, each carrying a trumpet, are to go in front of the Covenant Box. On the seventh day you and your soldiers are to march around the city seven times while the priests blow the trumpets. Then they are to sound one long note... all the people are to give a loud shout, and the city walls will collapse. Then the whole army will go straight into the city."

Joshua called the priests and told them, "Take the Covenant Box, and seven of you go in front of it, carrying trumpets." Then he ordered the people to start marching around the city, with an advance guard going on ahead of the Lord's Covenant Box.'

Something to think about

Jericho's wall was so thick you could have driven a car around the top of it. It seemed impossible to attack the city, but God was bigger and stronger than any city, fancy wall or army. The plan, however, seemed a bit bonkers. God wasn't going to send an earthquake or a mighty wind, or even just speak and make the wall disappear. No, He told Joshua to get the army to march around the city every day for a week – blowing trumpets. Talk about looking like a bunch of weirdos! Joshua trusted God, though. He didn't question it – he just got straight on with what God said to do.

Steve says...

Following God can sometimes mean doing things that no one else thinks will work. It was 12 years ago that God asked me to start Sorted, a magazine for men. At that time, sales of magazines were declining, I had no money to start up with and I had never done anything like it before. But I knew what God had asked, so I did it and it's still going now.

Something to talk about

· What's the craziest thing you've ever done?
· What made you do it?

Pray

Father God, help me to always follow You, even when it doesn't seem like the most obvious thing to do. Amen.

Impact

Joshua 6:15–17,20,25

'On the seventh day, they got up at daybreak and marched seven times round the city in the same way – this was the only day that they marched round it seven times. The seventh time around, when the priests were about to sound the trumpets, Joshua ordered the people to shout, and he said, "The LORD has given you the city! The city and everything in it must be totally destroyed as an offering to the LORD... Rahab and her household will be spared, because she hid our spies."...

So the priests blew the trumpets. As soon as the people heard it, they gave a loud shout, and the walls collapsed. Then the army went straight up the hill into the city and captured it... But Joshua spared the lives of... Rahab and all her relatives, because she had hidden the two spies that he had sent to Jericho.'

Something to think about

God's plan might have seemed bonkers, and His people might have felt a bit daft walking around the city every day with their trumpets, but God kept His promise and the walls came tumbling down. The mighty Jericho had fallen – all apart from Rahab, the woman who had recognised God and protected the spies. She and her family were saved and joined God's people.

Bekah says...

I love that Rahab's story doesn't end here. Her decision to do the right thing had an impact that lasted even beyond her lifetime. Her family became part of God's family that day and forever. In fact, if you read Matthew 1:5, you'll see that one day, far in the future, her great-great-great (and a lot more greats) grandson was Jesus. All because she made a good decision in Jericho.

Steve's amazing fact

Archaeologists' excavations of Jericho have shown it dates back to around 9000 BC, making it one of the earliest known cities. It's also said to have the oldest walls used for protection in the world, measuring an impressive 3.6 metres high and 1.8 metres (5.9 feet) wide. That is one seriously thick wall.

Something to talk about

· When have you made a decision that had big consequences?
· What helped you choose?

Pray

Father God, show me how to make wise decisions wherever I am and whatever I'm doing. Help me to remember that everything I do has consequences. Amen.

Choose

Joshua 24:13–15

'I gave you a land that you had never cultivated and cities that you had not built. Now you are living there and eating grapes from vines that you did not plant, and olives from trees that you did not plant.'

"Now then," Joshua continued, "honour the LORD and serve him sincerely and faithfully. Get rid of the gods which your ancestors used to worship in Mesopotamia and in Egypt, and serve only the LORD. If you are not willing to serve him, decide today whom you will serve, the gods your ancestors worshipped in Mesopotamia or the gods of the Amorites, in whose land you are now living. As for my family and me, we will serve the LORD."'

Something to think about

Over the next years, God enabled His people to take the land of Canaan, or Israel as it became known. Today, we're picking up the story at the end of that time – Joshua was getting old and knew he wouldn't be around much longer; he was giving his people one last message from God and some advice from himself. He reminded them of all God had done and then gave the Israelites a choice: they could worship the same things as all the people around them, or they could choose God. It was totally up to them. No one was going to make them follow God.

Bekah says...

God never makes us follow Him. Although they are not gods, many things – like money, TV, celebrities or computer games – can become objects of worship for some people. It can be tempting to make these things important in our lives too, but God gives us the same choice as Joshua gave the Israelites – 'decide today who you will serve'.

Something to talk about

· What things do you give a lot of time to in your life?
· How does that compare to the time you give God?

Pray

Dear God, our family chooses to serve You and follow wherever You lead us. Help us to give You the most time and thought. Amen.

Something for the weekend

Lots of families have the end of verse 15, 'As for my family and me, we will serve the LORD', on the wall in their house to show what decision they have made. We do. Why not create your own version and hang it up somewhere or stick it to your fridge?

Forgotten

Judges 2:11–15

'Then the people of Israel sinned against the LORD and began to serve the Baals. They stopped worshipping the LORD, the God of their ancestors, the God who had brought them out of Egypt, and they began to worship other gods, the gods of the peoples round them. They bowed down to them and made the LORD angry. They stopped worshipping the Lord and served the Baals and the Astartes. And so the Lord became furious with Israel and let raiders attack and rob them. He let enemies all around overpower them, and the Israelites could no longer protect themselves. Every time they went into battle, the LORD was against them, just as he had said he would be. They were in great distress.

Then the Lord gave the Israelites leaders who saved them from the raiders.'

Something to think about

God had been awesome and given the Israelites an amazing country, but it didn't take long for them to forget all about that and turn away from Him again. You can understand why the Bible tells us God was furious. His anger doesn't last forever though. He is the God of second chances, so He gave the Israelites new leaders, called judges, who heard God and had the power to save His people from their enemies.

Bekah says...

It's hard when we do something kind for people but they don't appreciate it or they ignore us and choose to be with other people, isn't it? Carrying on being kind can be difficult. Sometimes we need to stay away from people who hurt us, but being ready to give a second chance to someone who is genuinely sorry is really important.

Steve's amazing fact

Our minds are incredible. God certainly did a good job when he invented human beings. It's said that brain development begins in the womb, which could explain why babies recognise their mum's voice from the moment they're born.

Something to talk about

· When have you been good to someone but they haven't remembered it?
· How did you react?

Pray

Dear God, thank You for giving me a second chance, even when I sometimes forget You. Help me to love people the way You love me. Amen.

Girl power

Judges 4:4–9

'Now Deborah... was a prophet, and she was serving as a judge for the Israelites at that time. She used to sit under a certain palm tree... and the people of Israel would go there for her decisions. One day she sent for Barak son of Abinoam... and said to him, "The LORD, the God of Israel, has given you this command: 'Take 10,000 men from the tribes of Naphtali and Zebulun and lead them to Mount Tabor. I will bring Sisera, the commander of Jabin's army, to fight you at the River Kishon. He will have his chariots and soldiers, but I will give you victory over him.'"

Then Barak replied, "I will go if you go with me, but if you don't go with me, I won't go either."

She answered, "All right, I will go with you, but you won't get any credit for the victory, because the LORD will hand Sisera over to a woman."'

Something to think about

This would be an amazing story whoever the judge was, but it's especially incredible because this judge is a woman. God made Deborah the leader at a time when people thought girls weren't as good as boys, when women just did the cooking and looked after the home. But God created women to have the same gifts and talents as men, and He'd given lots of talents to Deborah! She was the leader of His people, a prophet who heard Him and passed on His messages, and she led an army that wouldn't go into battle without her. God's plan for Deborah was bigger than what other people thought women could do.

Steve's amazing fact

Despite not being allowed to go to Warsaw University because she was a girl, Marie Curie became a remarkable scientist who changed the world not once but twice. She pioneered the new science of radioactivity and her discoveries launched effective cancer treatment. She is still the only person to have won two Nobel Prizes in two different sciences.

Something to talk about

· Have you ever heard of people being treated badly because of the way they look or think?
· How does that make you feel?

Pray

Father God, help me not to judge other people and put limitations on them. Instead, please show me how to see them the way You do. Amen.

GI Jael

Judges 5:24–27

'The most fortunate of women is Jael,
  the wife of Heber the Kenite –
  the most fortunate of women who live in tents.
Sisera asked for water, but she gave him milk;
  she brought him cream in a beautiful bowl.
She took a tent peg in one hand,
  a worker's hammer in the other;
she struck Sisera and crushed his skull;
  she pierced him through the head.
He sank to his knees,
  fell down and lay still at her feet.
At her feet he sank to his knees and fell;
  he fell to the ground, dead.'

Something to think about

Now this story is a bit gruesome, but it shows another astonishing woman called Jael. She was at home in her tent, doing the housework, but the leader of the enemy came past and asked for water. Israel was at war with Sisera's people and now here he was, asking Jael for a drink. Sisera totally underestimated this lady, and that was a big mistake: Jael was incredibly strong, brave and able to do more than get him some water! Israel's army was being led by Deborah, and now Jael had won the battle for them.

Bekah says...

This story doesn't mean we should go around killing our enemies! It happened in a different time and place, before Jesus came to rescue the world. But it does mean we can do more than people think.

Years ago, someone told me that I'd made such a mess of my life I'd never be able do anything for God, but God had other plans. He has used me to tell all kinds of people about Jesus, in all kinds of ways. I don't need to pick up a hammer and tent peg to fight the enemy; I can do it by showing people who Jesus is.

Something to talk about

- Have you ever felt like you're not good enough to do something for God?
- What do you think He might have to say about that?

Pray

Dear God, thank You for having a plan to do more in my life than I can imagine. Help me to understand that with You anything is possible. Amen.

Strong, but rude

Judges 13:24; 14:1–3

'The woman gave birth to a son and named him Samson. The child grew and the LORD blessed him. And the LORD's power began to strengthen him...

One day Samson went down to Timnah, where he noticed a certain Philistine woman. He went back home and said to his father and mother, "There is a Philistine woman down at Timnah who has caught my attention. Get her for me; I want to marry her."

But his father and mother asked him, "Why do you have to go to those heathen Philistines to get a wife? Can't you find a girl in our own clan, among all our people?"

But Samson said to his father, "She is the one I want you to get for me. I like her."'

Something to think about

Samson was a special baby promised to his parents by God. The Bible tells us that God's Spirit rested on him and gave him a special strength. But that didn't make him very polite! Maybe Samson was a bit spoiled as an only child, or maybe he thought God's Spirit made him better than everyone else. Whatever the reason, the way he talked to his parents was just rude and demanding. No 'please's or 'thank you's, and no listening to their advice.

Bekah says...

Years before this, God had given His people the Ten Commandments, ten really important rules, and one of those was to respect your parents. It's hard sometimes, especially if they don't let us have or do what we want. But learning to speak kindly to our parents or carers - and our brothers and sisters - is super important and will lay the foundation for how we treat people all our lives.

Steve's amazing fact

Setting rules or boundaries for children is a really important thing for parents to do. Good, strong boundaries keep children safe from harm, help them develop healthy habits and even help them understand who they are and what they are responsible for.

Something to talk about

· How good are you at talking kindly to the people who look after you?
· In what ways could you try harder?

Pray

Father God, help us to respect everyone in our family and always speak kindly to them. Amen.

Superpowers!

Judges 15:12–15

'They said, "We have come here to tie you up, so we can hand you over to them."

Samson said, "Give me your word that you won't kill me yourselves."

"All right," they said, "we are only going to tie you up and hand you over to them. We won't kill you." So they tied him up with two new ropes and brought him back from the cliff.

When he got to Lehi, the Philistines came running toward him, shouting at him. Suddenly the power of the Lord made him strong, and he broke the ropes round his arms and hands as if they were burnt thread. Then he found the jawbone of a donkey that had recently died. He reached down and picked it up, and killed a thousand men with it.'

Something to think about

Samson was one of Israel's judges, and God gave him a superpower to fight the enemy. He must have been a bit like the Incredible Hulk – only he didn't go green. But he was probably just as scary to his enemies. In this story, Samson found himself in a situation where he was tied up and ready to be handed over to the enemy. But when they came, God's Spirit gave him the strength he needed to fight off a whole army! Amazing.

Bekah says...

This story is a bit of a one-off. God doesn't often give people the superpower of strength, but Jesus has promised to give us His Spirit, like Samson was given, and that Spirit gives us all different superpowers or 'gifts'. It might be as simple as the ability to love people who aren't very lovable, or to have great wisdom or be really good at hearing God's voice.

Steve's amazing fact

Whenever a rope is tied, it is weakened. Tests show that the place where a rope usually breaks it at the knot. If you do need to tie a knot in a rope, the strongest is the figure-eight follow-through.

Something to talk about

· What gifts or superpowers has God given you?
· What gifts or superpowers has God given the other people in your family?

Pray

Holy Spirit, please give us more of Your power now so that we can be more like Jesus in what we do and say. Amen.

WEEK 3
LEADERS WITH A
DIFFERENCE
WEEKEND

It's not over yet

Judges 16:28–30

'Then Samson prayed, "Sovereign LORD, please remember me; please, God, give me my strength just once more, so that with this one blow I can get even with the Philistines for putting out my two eyes." So Samson took hold of the two middle pillars holding up the building. Putting one hand on each pillar, he pushed against them and shouted, "Let me die with the Philistines!" He pushed with all his might, and the building fell down on the five kings and everyone else. Samson killed more people at his death than he had killed during his life.'

Something to think about

Samson spent years fighting Israel's enemies and, after his wife tricked him and cut his hair, his enemies finally captured him, blinded him and tied him up. The king had brought him into one of his big celebrations to publicly show off that he had beaten the mighty Samson and his God. But it wasn't the end of the story: Samson had one last fight left in him, and God gave him power once again to fight the enemy. We might think we've reached the end and run out of time, but God can always add another chapter.

Bekah says...

I heard a story about a famous church leader called D.L. Moody who had a list of 100 people who he prayed for every day. His prayers were his way of fighting the enemy because he prayed these people would become Christians. By the time he died, 96 of them had chosen to follow Jesus. At his funeral, the last four people did too.

Steve says...

Like Samson, I had a really bad, short haircut once and my boss at the bank where I worked was far from impressed. I was lucky that, generally, the hair on your head grows about half an inch per month (that's six inches per year) and I didn't get into too much trouble.

Something to talk about

· Have you ever given up on something because you thought it was too late?
· Is there something you need to give one last try?

Pray

Dear Lord Jesus, I want all my friends and family to know You. Please help me and others to tell them about You. Amen.

Something for the weekend

Why not write a list of people that you, as a family, can pray for? It doesn't have to be 100 people like D.L. Moody, but it's a great way to fight for Jesus and it will be exciting to see what happens!

Teased and misunderstood

1 Samuel 1:2–8

'Elkanah had two wives, Hannah and Peninnah. Peninnah had children, but Hannah had none. Every year Elkanah went from Ramah to worship and offer sacrifices to the Lord Almighty at Shiloh... Each time Elkanah offered his sacrifice, he would give one share of the meat to Peninnah and one share to each of her children. And even though he loved Hannah very much he would give her only one share, because the Lord had kept her from having children. Peninnah, her rival, would torment and humiliate her, because the Lord had kept her childless. This went on year after year; whenever they went to the house of the Lord, Peninnah would upset Hannah so much that she would cry and refuse to eat anything. Her husband Elkanah would ask her, "Hannah, why are you crying? Why won't you eat? Why are you always so sad? Don't I mean more to you than ten sons?"'

Something to think about

Hannah had a tough time. For starters, she shared a husband with another woman. On top of that, the other wife, Peninnah, had children and Hannah didn't. To make things even worse, Peninnah was horrible about it and teased Hannah. The Bible doesn't tell us what she said, but you can imagine her gloating about her children and being insensitive to Hannah's heartache of being childless. Really, Peninnah was bullying Hannah, and their husband didn't actually try to stop it; instead of listening to Hannah and supporting her, he kept telling her that she was being a bit silly getting so upset. Not very helpful.

Steve says...

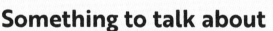

Bullying is no laughing matter. I used to take an anti-bullying roadshow into schools and explain to children how they can tackle bullying by becoming a HERO. H stands for 'Help Out' – talk to the bully or chat to the victim about what's happening. 'E' is for 'Empathise' – try to understand how the person being bullied feels. R is for 'Report' – tell an adult. 'O' is for 'Open Communication' – no-one should be afraid to talk about bullying and what can be done to stop it.

Something to talk about

· Have you ever been bullied by someone?
· How did you deal with that?

Pray

Father God, please help us to look out for people who are being bullied at school or at work and to never ever join in. Amen.

Still misunderstood!

1 Samuel 1:9–17

'[Hannah] was deeply distressed, and she cried bitterly as she prayed to the LORD. Meanwhile, Eli the priest was sitting in his place by the door. Hannah made a solemn promise: "Almighty LORD, look at me, your servant!... If you give me a son, I promise that I will dedicate him to you for his whole life and that he will never have his hair cut."

Hannah continued... and Eli watched her lips. She was praying silently; her lips were moving, but she made no sound. So Eli thought that she was drunk, and said to her, "Stop making a drunken show of yourself... sober up!"

"No, I'm not drunk, sir," she answered. "I haven't been drinking! I am desperate, and I have been praying, pouring out my troubles to the LORD... because I'm so miserable."

"Go in peace," Eli said, "and may the God of Israel give you what you have asked him for."'

Something to think about

Poor Hannah. Her husband hadn't really listened, so now she's gone to the Temple to tell God about her sadness, and the priest thinks she's drunk! Everyone misunderstood her, but she didn't let it rest. She politely explained to Eli the priest that she was just sad and desperate for God to hear her prayer. Eli listened and shared her prayer to God for her to have a baby of her own. What a difference it makes when someone really listens to us.

Bekah says...

I hate being misunderstood. When I was a little girl I used to speak really quickly and lots of people didn't understand what I was trying to say, sometimes not even my mum. I'd come home from school with exciting stories to tell, and she'd tell me to stop and start again. It made me so frustrated!

Steve's amazing fact

The Yucatan Peninsula in Mexico is said to have got its name because of a misunderstanding. The story goes that when the first Spanish explorers arrived and asked what the place was called, the natives answered with a word like 'Yucatan', which actually meant 'I don't understand you'. Hilariously, the name stuck.

Something to talk about

· Do you ever feel like people just don't understand you?
· Who do you think does listen to you well, and how does that make you feel?

Pray

Dear Lord Jesus, thank You for really knowing me better than I know myself. I'm so grateful that I can always talk to You. Amen.

Grateful

1 Samuel 1:19–22

'the LORD answered her prayer. So it was that she became pregnant and gave birth to a son. She named him Samuel, and explained, "I asked the LORD for him."

The time came again for Elkanah and his family to go to Shiloh and offer to the LORD the yearly sacrifice and the special sacrifice he had promised. But this time Hannah did not go. She told her husband, "As soon as the child is weaned, I will take him to the house of the LORD, where he will stay all his life."'

Something to think about

Hannah got her longed-for baby and she gave him a special name. She knew it was more than luck that she got pregnant, and it wasn't just biology. This baby was a gift from God so she called him Samuel, which means 'heard by God'. At the time, it was an unusual name to call a baby, but actually it shows that Hannah could see God at work in her life. When good things happen, it's really easy to just be pleased about them and then move on, but it's good to stop and see what God's doing in our lives, and thank Him for the gifts He gives us.

Bekah says...

It's not just the big things God gives us that it's good to thank Him for. I travelled to Kenya a few years ago to work with a church out there. The people amazed me with their prayers. Every time someone prayed, they started with, 'Thank You, God, that I woke up this morning.' To start with, I thought this was a weird thing to say, but I soon realised that actually it was perfect. These lovely people knew how to be grateful for even the breath God gave them. Remembering everything was a gift from God made them really happy, even though they were very poor.

Steve's amazing fact

Apparently, being grateful is actually good for your health. According to a 2012 study, grateful people felt fewer aches and pains, and on the whole said they felt healthier than other people.

Something to talk about

· When has God given you something amazing?
· Why not list some of the more ordinary but amazing things that God has given you today?

Pray

Dear God, You give us so many gifts. Please help us to be like Hannah and always remember to be grateful. Amen.

Dedicated

1 Samuel 1:23–24,26–28

'So Hannah stayed at home and nursed her child.

After she had weaned him... she took Samuel, young as he was, to the house of the LORD at Shiloh... Hannah said to [Eli], "Excuse me, sir. Do you remember me? I am the woman you saw standing here, praying to the LORD. I asked him for this child, and he gave me what I asked for. So I am dedicating him to the LORD. As long as he lives, he will belong to the LORD."

Then they worshipped the LORD there.'

Something to think about

When she was praying to God in the Temple, Hannah had made a big promise to Him. She'd said that if God let her get pregnant then she would dedicate the child to God. That's a pretty big promise – and she kept it. Samuel lived in the temple with Eli from then on, and Hannah only visited him. As much as Hannah had wanted a baby, she knew Samuel was a gift and she wanted to show God that she appreciated it. She wanted Him to share in this special boy.

Bekah says...

Hannah had learned not to make anything more important than God. Not even her son. We might have all kinds of things that are precious to us, and we can dedicate those things to God by finding ways of using them for Him. It might mean inviting people round for dinner, letting other kids play with our toys, or using our musical gifts during a church service.

Steve says...

Some Christian families have special services to dedicate their children to God. That doesn't mean they leave their children to grow up in the church without them. The parents are showing God they are grateful for their children and promising to keep God as part of the family so that their children grow up knowing Him.

Something to talk about

· Did you have any special ceremonies when you were born?
· Do you know what the importance of these were?

Pray

Dear God, thank You for all the good things You have given me. I want You to be the most important thing in my life. Help me to use my gifts for You. Amen.

Blessed

1 Samuel 2:18–21

'In the meantime the boy Samuel continued to serve the LORD, wearing a sacred linen apron. Each year his mother would make a little robe and take it to him when she accompanied her husband to offer the yearly sacrifice. Then Eli would bless Elkanah and his wife, and say to Elkanah, "May the LORD give you other children by this woman to take the place of the one you dedicated to him."

After that they would go back home.

The LORD did bless Hannah, and she had three more sons and two daughters. The boy Samuel grew up in the service of the LORD.'

Something to think about

Hannah really trusted God. She trusted him enough to let Him have the thing most important to her. She didn't know He'd give her more children. What she did know was that He was good and that He was all she needed, even if she never had more children. That's pretty amazing faith, and God blessed her for it. We can't begin to imagine how hard it must have been to leave Samuel behind each year. But God saw how much Hannah loved him, and gave her more children to love. She ended up with a great big family.

Bekah says...

So often we think we need more things to make us happy – whether that's a bigger house, a better car or the latest game or gadget. Learning that God is all we need is really hard, but it means we can be happy wherever we are, no matter what's going on.

Steve says...

I've had the honour of travelling to many different countries with Operation Christmas Child and have seen for myself how a simple shoebox gift, sent with love, can have a huge impact. It's so humbling to see a little box packed with small things – a toy, bar of soap, toothbrush and tennis ball – bringing such joy to disadvantaged children around the world.

Something to talk about

· What things do you think would make you happier?
· What are the things that you actually need in your life?

Pray

Dear Lord Jesus, there are so many things that I'd love to have, but help me to remember that the most important things in my life are You and my family. Amen.

Strange voice

1 Samuel 3:2–8

'One night Eli, who was now almost blind, was sleeping in his own room; Samuel was sleeping in the sanctuary, where the sacred Covenant Box was. Before dawn, while the lamp was still burning, the LORD called Samuel. He answered, "Yes, sir!" and ran to Eli and said, "You called me, and here I am."

But Eli answered, "I didn't call you; go back to bed." So Samuel went back to bed.

The LORD called Samuel again. The boy did not know that it was the LORD, because the LORD had never spoken to him before. So he got up, went to Eli, and said, "You called me, and here I am."

But Eli answered, "My son, I didn't call you; go back to bed."

The LORD called Samuel a third time; he got up, went to Eli, and said, "You called me, and here I am."

Then Eli realized that it was the LORD who was calling the boy'

Something to think about

When you stop to think about it, it's amazing that God chooses to speak to humans. Samuel didn't even realise it was God speaking. He needed his wiser, older friend Eli to help him recognise God's voice. The Bible tells us that Samuel went on to become a prophet – listening to God for other people too.

God still speaks to us, but it's easy to be like Samuel and miss it. He speaks to us through His Word (the Bible), maybe by a verse we remember just when we need it; sometimes through dreams or pictures; and sometimes through thoughts in our heads, like God is whispering to our hearts.

Something to talk about

· When have you heard God speak to you?
· How were you sure it was Him?

Pray

Father God, I want to hear Your voice. Please speak to me and help me to hear You above all the noise. Amen.

Something for the weekend

Could you practise listening to God together? Take five minutes to sit together in silence for a while so you can hear His voice. God always sounds like love, so this can help you tell the difference between His voice and your thoughts. You might not all hear God, so share with each other what you do hear and don't worry if one of you doesn't hear Him this time.

Appointed

1 Kings 2:1–4

'When David was about to die, he called his son Solomon and gave him his last instructions: "My time to die has come. Be confident and determined, and do what the LORD your God orders you to do. Obey all his laws and commands, as written in the Law of Moses, so that wherever you go you may prosper in everything you do. If you obey him, the LORD will keep the promise he made when he told me that my descendants would rule Israel as long as they were careful to obey his commands faithfully with all their heart and soul.'

Something to think about

Much later in his life, God told Samuel to anoint a shepherd boy called David to be king of Israel. He's the guy who fought the giant and went on to do amazing things, and he's described in the Bible as a man who sought after God's heart. David really loved God. He made mistakes along the way, but he always wanted the Israelites to follow and worship God. David had lots of children, but God told him that actually it was his tenth son who would be the next king – Solomon. The last message David had for Solomon wasn't about how to conquer other lands or rule the country. It wasn't even about how to look after the family. The most important thing David wanted to tell Solomon was to always follow God and His rules, just as David had learnt.

Bekah says...

My granny and grandpa died a long time ago, but I still remember some of the pieces of wisdom they gave me. Things like, 'Count the pennies and the pounds will look after themselves.' Or, 'When you choose your friends, the most important quality in a person is kindness.'

Steve's amazing fact

David was the eighth (and youngest) son of Jesse, from the tribe of Judah. He became king at the age of 30, and his reign went on for 40 years. After dying from natural causes around 970 BC, he was buried in Jerusalem.

Something to talk about

- Grown-ups, if you had one thing you wanted your children to remember, what would that be?
- Children, what's the most important piece of advice you've been given?

Pray

God, there are so many things I could talk about each day, so help me to say the important stuff and pass on good messages to others. Amen.

Question and answer

1 Kings 3:5–9

'The LORD appeared to [Solomon] in a dream and asked him, "What would you like me to give you?"

Solomon answered, "You always showed great love for my father David, your servant, and he was good, loyal, and honest in his relation with you. And you have continued to show him your great and constant love by giving him a son who today rules in his place. O LORD God, you have let me succeed my father as king, even though I am very young and don't know how to rule. Here I am among the people you have chosen to be your own, a people who are so many that they cannot be counted. So give me the wisdom I need to rule your people with justice and to know the difference between good and evil. Otherwise, how would I ever be able to rule this great people of yours?"'

Something to think about

At this point in the story, God seems a little bit like the genie in the film *Aladdin*. He granted Solomon a wish. What do you think you would ask for? It would be so easy to get carried away with all the things we want. But Solomon remembered who he was speaking to – the King of kings and Lord of lords – and he knew how awesome it was that he had been made king of Israel. It was a gift. He wasn't puffed up with pride; instead he knew he couldn't do a good job on his own. So he asked for the best thing he could: the wisdom to be a good king.

Steve says...

We all have dreams, and these vary incredibly from person to person. Some of us dream of being movie stars, some of us dream of going into space, and others of us wish to one day be world-famous rock stars. While we each have our own specific goals, there are also many dreams and wishes that are common to most of us. Lots of people really want good health, money, love, peace, freedom or just to be happy.

Something to talk about

· If you had one wish, what would it be?
· Why?

Pray

Dear Lord, You give such good gifts to us. Help us to be really wise with what we ask for. Amen.

Problem

1 Kings 3:17–22

'One of [the women] said, "Your Majesty, this woman and
I live in the same house, and I gave birth to a baby boy at
home while she was there. Two days after my child was
born, she also gave birth to a baby boy... Then one night
she accidentally rolled over on her baby and smothered
it. She got up during the night, took my son from my side
while I was asleep, and carried him to her bed; then she put
the dead child in my bed. The next morning, when I woke
up and was going to feed my baby, I saw that it was dead. I
looked at it more closely and saw that it was not my child."

But the other woman said, "No! The living child is mine,
and the dead one is yours!"...

And so they argued before the king.'

Something to think about

What a dilemma! And what a sad situation – two mums
fighting, and one of them had lost her baby. It's easy to
think that one of them is just being terrible but actually,
when we're very sad we sometimes do things we wouldn't
normally do at all. Solomon's wisdom had become famous;
he was incredible at knowing the right thing to do. So these
ladies had come to ask him to sort out their problem. How
would you decide who was telling the truth?

Bekah says...

We have five girls, and we've fostered and looked after more children too. Over the years, we've certainly had a lot of disagreements to sort out over broken toys, games that have been played 'wrong' and people who've felt left out. Working out what has really happened is not always easy.

Steve says...

When I was little, my Uncle Harry used to tell me that when the ice cream van's music played, it meant that they'd completely sold out of ice cream. It took me years to figure out he wasn't telling the truth!

Something to talk about

· When have you had a really tough time working out who was telling the truth?
· How did you work it out?

Pray

Father God, it's horrible when two people are saying different things and we have to work out the truth. Help us to have wisdom like Solomon. Amen.

Solved

1 Kings 3:23–28

'Then King Solomon said, "Each of you claims that the living child is hers and that the dead child belongs to the other one." He sent for a sword, and when it was brought, he said, "Cut the living child in two and give each woman half of it."

The real mother, her heart full of love for her son, said to the king, "Please, Your Majesty, don't kill the child! Give it to her!"

But the other woman said, "Don't give it to either of us; go ahead and cut it in two."

Then Solomon said, "Don't kill the child! Give it to the first woman – she is its real mother."

When the people of Israel heard of Solomon's decision, they were all filled with deep respect for him, because they knew then that God had given him the wisdom to settle disputes fairly.'

Something to think about

Solomon's way of sorting out the problem seemed very extreme, but he was never really going to cut the baby in half. He always knew that saying this would make the real mother speak out, or the other mother show herself to be lying. The king was using his gift of wisdom to help other people and to bring fairness to the country. When we have talents, it's good to use them for God and to bless other people.

Bekah says...

When I was younger, I was a pretty good pianist and I loved just playing by myself in my own little world. But as my sister grew up and started learning the flute, I realised it could really help her if we played our instruments together. Then we started playing at church too.

Steve says...

I became an expert on the pogo stick when I was 11 years old, all because of a girl called Gillian who moved into my street. She joined my class at school, and me and my mates wanted to impress her when we played out in our road. We all became amazing pogo-stickers that summer, but Gillian was suitably unimpressed.

Something to talk about
· What talents do you have?
· How could you use them to bless other people?

Pray

Dear Lord Jesus, thank You for giving me skills and talents of my own. I want to use them to bless other people – please help me. Amen.

A Temple for the Lord

1 Kings 6:1,11–14,38

'Four hundred and eighty years after the people of Israel left Egypt, during the fourth year of Solomon's reign over Israel, in the second month, the month of Ziv, Solomon began work on the Temple....

The LORD said to Solomon, "If you obey all my laws and commands, I will do for you what I promised your father David. I will live among my people Israel in this Temple that you are building, and I will never abandon them."

So Solomon finished building the Temple...

In the eighth month, the month of Bul, in the eleventh year of Solomon's reign, the Temple was completely finished exactly as it had been planned. It had taken Solomon seven years to build it.'

Something to think about

Solomon started well. One of the first things he did in his reign was build a temple for God. Ever since God's people escaped from Egypt, they had carried a special box called the Ark of the Covenant around with them and put up a tent wherever they settled for it to be placed in. God didn't live in the box or the tent, but it was a special place where He would meet priests when they entered. Solomon built the Temple to create a permanent place where God's people could meet with Him. It showed that the Israelites were no longer wandering around; they were in their proper home and God was with them. Solomon was making sure God was right at the heart of the country.

Bekah says...

We don't need special places to meet with God anymore. Sometimes we have quiet or beautiful places where we find it easier to remember that God is with us, but when Jesus came and died, He made it possible for anyone to meet with God, anywhere and anytime. All we have to do is ask.

Something to talk about

· Do you have a special place where you feel close to God?
· How does it feel to know God is always with you?

Pray

Father God, thank You that I can meet with You anywhere I go. I don't need to be in a special place or time to be in Your presence. Amen.

Divided

1 Kings 11:9–13

'Even though the Lord, the God of Israel, had appeared to Solomon twice and had commanded him not to worship foreign gods, Solomon did not obey the LORD but turned away from him. So the LORD was angry with Solomon and said to him, "Because you have deliberately broken your covenant with me and disobeyed my commands, I promise that I will take the kingdom away from you and give it to one of your officials. However, for the sake of your father David I will not do this in your lifetime, but during the reign of your son. And I will not take the whole kingdom away from him; instead, I will leave him one tribe for the sake of my servant David and for the sake of Jerusalem, the city I have made my own."'

Something to think about

Solomon was given great wisdom, but he didn't always use it. As the years went by and God blessed him with riches and great power, it all began to go to his head. He had hundreds of wives and they took a lot of his attention away from God and being a good king. Some of those wives worshipped fake gods, and Solomon started to do the same to please them.

He had started so well, but he had forgotten the real God who had given him everything in the first place –

and the consequences were terrible. Because of his poor leadership, he was the last king of all Israel. He left it in such a mess that, just after his death, it split into two separate countries: Judah and Israel. What a shame!

Steve says...

I do comedy magic shows, tricks and illusions that give me an opportunity to talk to people about Jesus, and over the years I have done over 4,000 shows in 30 different countries. On one occasion, I turned up at a show in Surrey and opened the boot of my car to get my props out, to discover I hadn't put them in! Oh man, that was a tough gig.

Something to talk about
· When have you forgotten something important?
· What helps you remember things?

Pray
Dear Lord Jesus, You are a great God. I don't want to forget that or get distracted by other things. Please help me stay focused on You. Amen.

Something for the weekend
Why not make a memory box of things that are important to you as a family? It could include trinkets or notes that help you remember happy times and special moments.

Danger

1 Kings 17:1–6

'A prophet named Elijah, from Tishbe in Gilead, said to King Ahab, "In the name of the LORD, the living God of Israel, whom I serve, I tell you that there will be no dew or rain for the next two or three years until I say so."

Then the LORD said to Elijah, "Leave this place and go east and hide yourself near the brook of Cherith, east of the Jordan. The brook will supply you with water to drink, and I have commanded ravens to bring you food there."

Elijah obeyed the LORD's command, and went and stayed by Cherith Brook. He drank water from the brook, and ravens brought him bread and meat every morning and every evening.'

Something to think about

Hundreds of years after Samuel carried messages from God to His people, Elijah came along to do something similar. The Bible doesn't tell us about Elijah's childhood, only where he came from. He lived at a time when Israel was ruled by a terrible king. In fact, 1 Kings 16:33 tells us that Ahab was the worst king Israel ever had. It didn't help that Ahab was married to Queen Jezebel – a woman who tried to get rid of all God's priests and prophets and make God's people worship a statue called Baal.

It was a tough time to be God's messenger. Telling the king that God wasn't happy with him and that there wasn't going to be any rain for years wouldn't just make Elijah unpopular, it was downright dangerous. God had a plan to take care of his prophet though – to keep him safe.

Bekah says...

It's easy to think that following God should be a bit like having a fairy godmother or a genie who grants all our wishes, when in reality, doing God's work can be tough and sometimes scary. But we can always know that God has a plan to take care of us too, even if His mission for us is going to take courage.

Something to talk about

· Has following God ever been a bit uncomfortable for you?
· What helped you follow Him anyway?

Pray

Dear Lord, I want to follow You, even when it's tough. Help me to remember that You'll always be there for me like You were for Elijah. Amen.

Partnership

1 Kings 17:7–16

'After a while the brook dried up because of the lack of rain.
    Then the LORD said to Elijah, "Now go to the town of
Zarephath... I have commanded a widow who lives there
to feed you." So Elijah went... he saw a widow gathering
firewood. "Please bring me a drink of water," he said to her...
"And please bring me some bread, too."
    She answered, "By the living LORD your God I swear that
I haven't got any bread. All I have is a handful of flour in a
bowl and a drop of olive oil in a jar. I came here to gather
some firewood to take back home and prepare what little I
have for my son and me... then we will starve to death."
    "Don't worry," Elijah said to her. "Go ahead and prepare
your meal. But first make a small loaf from what you have
and bring it to me, and then prepare the rest for you and
your son. For this is what the LORD, the God of Israel, says:
'The bowl will not run out of flour or the jar run out of oil
before the day that I, the LORD, send rain.'"'

Something to think about

Elijah had known that God was protecting and providing for
him, and it would have reassured him that he had done the
right thing when he delivered the message to the king. But
the brook drying up could have ended all that certainty;

Elijah might have thought God had forgotten him after all. But God hadn't – He had a new plan. It involved another of God's people, someone who thought she had nothing to give: a lady who had already lost her husband and now thought that she and her son were about to starve to death too. God had other plans though – to provide for her, her son and Elijah – if she did things His way.

Steve's amazing fact

According to the Guinness Book of Records, the worst drought ever recorded happened in China between 1876 and 1879. Estimates are that between 9 and 13 million people died in northern China when the rains failed to come for a staggering three whole years.

Something to talk about

- Have you ever thought that you have nothing to offer someone who needs help?
- What do you think God might say about that?

Pray

Dear God, I don't always feel like I have much to offer, but I want to be ready to help people anyway. Please help me. Amen.

God comes through

1 Kings 17:15–22

'The widow went and did as Elijah had told her, and all of them had enough food for many days...

Some time later the widow's son got sick; he got worse and worse, and finally he died. She said to Elijah, "Man of God, why did you do this to me? Did you come here to remind God of my sins and so cause my son's death?"

"Give the boy to me," Elijah said. He took the boy from her arms, carried him upstairs to the room where he was staying, and laid him on the bed. Then he prayed aloud, "O LORD my God, why have you done such a terrible thing to this widow? She has been kind enough to take care of me, and now you kill her son!" Then Elijah stretched himself out on the boy three times and prayed, "O LORD my God, restore this child to life!" The LORD answered Elijah's prayer; the child started breathing again and revived.'

Something to think about

Elijah was really good at hearing God and following Him, but it wasn't always easy. The brook ran out of water, and once God fixed that, something far worse happened: the woman's son died. She confronted Elijah about it, and Elijah talked to God about what was going on – why was He letting this happen?

It's good to know that it's OK to question God when things are tough. But Elijah doesn't just complain. He knows that the only way through this tough time is *with* God, so he prays and he asks for a miracle. What happens? God comes through – again!

Bekah says

I love that it's OK to tell God when we're not happy or we don't understand where He is. King David wrote songs to help him express how he felt during these times. One of them is Psalm 22.

Steve's amazing fact

Miracles – events that are caused by God and don't follow the laws of nature – run throughout the Bible. In fact, there are at least 126 recorded in both the Old and New Testaments combined. Without them the Bible would be a much slimmer book.

Something to talk about

· When has your life been tough?
· How easy did you find it to pray during that time?

Pray

Father God, when times are tough, I want to remember to talk to You about it – to tell You what's going wrong and to ask You for Your help. Amen.

Courage

1 Kings 18:18–21

"'I'm not the troublemaker," Elijah answered. "You are – you and your father. You are disobeying the LORD's commands and worshipping the idols of Baal. Now order all the people of Israel to meet me at Mount Carmel. Bring along the 450 prophets of Baal and the 400 prophets of the goddess Asherah who are supported by Queen Jezebel."

So Ahab summoned all the Israelites and the prophets of Baal to meet at Mount Carmel. Elijah went up to the people and said, "How much longer will it take you to make up your minds? If the LORD is God, worship him; but if Baal is God, worship him!" But the people didn't say a word.'

Something to think about

Time went by. There was no rain and life was getting harder and harder for the Israelites, and for King Ahab and Queen Jezebel. Finally God was ready to make a move and he sent Elijah to set up a showdown between Him and the statue gods Baal and Asherah. The plan sounded great, but it meant Elijah had to go back to the palace with another unpopular message. He told the king it was his fault that there had been no rain. Next he asked all the prophets and priests of the statue gods to come to Mount Carmel to meet him. Then he challenged the Israelites to think about who they really wanted to follow.

Bekah says...

Elijah was super brave and spoke the truth to people. It's easy to tell people what they want to hear, but sometimes if we really love them we need to kindly say things that aren't so popular. We might need to tell a person we don't think what they're doing is right, or that their idea isn't very wise, or that they can't do what they want. It's not easy but it is important sometimes.

Steve's amazing fact

Mount Carmel isn't just one peak. It's actually an entire mountain range in northern Israel. Its highest point is the steep ridge on the north-eastern side, which is more than 500 metres tall. The mountain range is made up of flint and limestone, contains several caves and grows oak, pine and olive trees.

Something to talk about

· When have you had to tell somebody something tough?
· How did you feel?

Pray

God, I want to be a truth speaker even when it's hard.
Help me to always be kind, but also true. Amen.

Statue gods

1 Kings 18:25–29

'Then Elijah said to the prophets of Baal, "Since there are so many of you, you take a bull and prepare it first. Pray to your god, but don't set fire to the wood."

They took the bull that was brought to them, prepared it, and prayed to Baal until noon. They shouted, "Answer us, Baal!" and kept dancing round the altar they had built. But no answer came.

At noon Elijah started making fun of them: "Pray louder! He is a god! Maybe he is daydreaming or relieving himself, or perhaps he's gone on a journey! Or maybe he's sleeping, and you've got to wake him up!" So the prophets prayed louder and cut themselves with knives and daggers, according to their ritual, until blood flowed. They kept on ranting and raving until the middle of the afternoon; but no answer came, not a sound was heard.'

Something to think about

The showdown was set up. Two bulls would be killed ready to become two burnt sacrifices – one to Baal, the statue god, and one to the real God of Israel. But no human would light the fires beneath the bulls. Instead, the prophets would ask their god to light the fire for them, and Elijah would ask the real God to light the fire for him. Elijah even let the Baal prophets go first and they spent the whole afternoon getting into a frenzy, asking Baal to start the blaze. He didn't, of course, because he's not real.

Bekah says...

Most people don't worship statues or sacrifice bulls anymore, but we do often think things other than God will solve all our problems. We think money, popularity or being clever will make us happy, and sometimes (a bit like those Baal prophets) we end up frantically chasing these things when actually the only one that can bring us lasting joy is God.

Something to talk about

· What things do you think you need in order to have a good life?
· Where does God fit into your list?

Pray

Dear God, I'm sorry for the times when I focus on the wrong things. Help me to look to You for my happiness and not to worry so much about money and friends and being the cleverest. Amen.

Showing God off

1 Kings 18:30–37

'Then Elijah said to the people, "Come closer to me," and they all gathered round him. He rebuilt the altar for the worship of the LORD. He dug a trench round it... Then he placed the wood on the altar, cut the bull in pieces, and laid it on the wood. He said, "Fill four jars with water and pour it on the offering and the wood." They did so, and he said, "Do it again" – and they did. "Do it once more," he said – and they did. The water ran down round the altar and filled the trench...

Elijah approached the altar and prayed, "O LORD, the God of Abraham, Isaac, and Jacob, prove now that you are the God of Israel and that I am your servant and have done all this at your command. Answer me, LORD, answer me, so that this people will know that you, the LORD, are God, and that you are bringing them back to yourself."'

Something to think about

Instead of just praying to God, Elijah made his challenge harder, soaking everything with water! It would take a real miracle to get this soggy pile of wood alight! So, Elijah stepped up to pray to God in front of everyone. Can you imagine how much pressure that would have been? So many people were watching him, most of them hated him, some of them wanted him dead, but Elijah knew who his God was and what he knew gave him the courage to stand and ask God to once again show up.

Steve says...

What I love about this story is that Elijah wasn't showing himself off, he was showing God off. Everything he did was to remind people how great God was and help them choose to follow Him again.

Something to talk about

· When has God done something out of the ordinary in your life?
· How did that make you feel?

Pray

Dear God, help me to show other people how amazing You are and not just keep You to myself. Amen.

Something for the weekend

We don't need to make sacrifices like this anymore, but we can still show people how amazing God is by telling them the wonderful things He's done in our lives. Why not work out some stories you as a family can tell people, and maybe even invite these people over to talk about Jesus?

Consequences

1 Kings 18:38–41

'The LORD sent fire down, and it burnt up the sacrifice, the wood, and the stones, scorched the earth and dried up the water in the trench. When the people saw this, they threw themselves on the ground and exclaimed, "The LORD is God; the LORD alone is God!"

Elijah ordered, "Seize the prophets of Baal; don't let any of them get away!" The people seized them all, and Elijah led them down to the River Kishon and killed them.

Then Elijah said to King Ahab, "Now, go and eat. I hear the roar of rain approaching."'

Something to think about

There is something amazing and something a bit frightening about this part of the story. God showed up and set the altar alight, even though everything was soaking wet. Even more amazing than that, the Israelites remembered who God was and chose to worship Him. But there were some who saw what God did, saw how awesome He was and how rubbish Baal was, yet still chose to worship Baal. It's hard to understand why they made that decision, and it had pretty terrible consequences.

Bekah says...

It's not something we like to think about, but God had given these prophets a front row seat to His miracle, yet they chose to ignore Him. Every decision we make has consequences, big or small. The Bible tells us that, like the prophets of Baal, we also get to choose whether we follow God or not. One day, there will be consequences to our choice – we either live with God forever or we get sent away from Him. I know where I'd rather be; do you?

Steve's amazing fact

The strongest tropical cyclone ever happened on 12 October 1979 in the Pacific. Typhoon Tip is remembered for both its incredible intensity and size. Tip's diameter spanned approximately 1,380 miles! It eventually weakened as it made landfall in south Japan five days later, but it still had devastating effects.

Something to talk about

· What's the best decision you've ever made?
· What are some of the reasons people choose not to follow Jesus?

Pray

Father God, You are so awesome. You can do anything, and still You give us the choice to follow You or not. I choose to follow You today and always. Amen.

Let there be rain!

1 Kings 18:42–45

'While Ahab went to eat, Elijah climbed to the top of Mount Carmel, where he bowed down to the ground, with his head between his knees. He said to his servant, "Go and look toward the sea."

The servant went and returned, saying, "I didn't see anything." Seven times in all Elijah told him to go and look. The seventh time he returned and said, "I saw a little cloud no bigger than a man's hand, coming up from the sea."

Elijah ordered his servant, "Go to King Ahab and tell him to get into his chariot and go back home before the rain stops him."

In a little while the sky was covered with dark clouds, the wind began to blow, and heavy rain began to fall. Ahab got into his chariot and started back to Jezreel.'

Something to think about

Sometimes we have to wait. Israel hadn't had rain for years, and now the time was nearly here. The people had chosen to follow God again and so God was going to keep His promise, like always. Elijah and his servant just needed to be patient. The servant wasn't sure, though, and kept coming back to say he couldn't see any clouds. You can imagine him getting a bit fed up of going to look, and maybe he started to panic that the rain would never come after all. But Elijah knew.

Elijah knew His God so well – he'd been brave for God before, he'd been fed by God before, he'd even raised a boy from the dead with God before. Elijah knew God could bring the rain and so he kept saying, 'Look again.' God doesn't always do things quite how we expect or when we expect, but he always keeps His promises.

Bekah says...

Being patient means being able to accept annoying situations and problems without getting worked up about them. Easier said than done! We all tease Steve for being super impatient – whether he's waiting in a queue at a shop, driving in the car or trying to get us all out of the house on time.

Something to talk about
· When have you had to be patient?
· How easy do you find it to wait for things?

Pray
Father God, I'm sorry for the times I get impatient. Please help me to be better at waiting for good things without moaning. Amen.

An ordinary superhero

1 Kings 19:1–5

'King Ahab told his wife Jezebel everything that Elijah had done and how he had put all the prophets of Baal to death. She sent a message to Elijah: "May the gods strike me dead if by this time tomorrow I don't do the same thing to you that you did to the prophets." Elijah was afraid, and fled for his life; he took his servant and went to Beersheba in Judah.

Leaving the servant there, Elijah walked a whole day into the wilderness. He stopped and sat down in the shade of a tree and wished he would die. "It's too much, LORD," he prayed. "Take away my life; I might as well be dead!"

He lay down under the tree and fell asleep.'

Something to think about

This is a really interesting part of the story. We know Elijah knew God. We know Elijah had seen God do amazing things. But he had been through a lot, and Jezebel threatening to kill him was one thing too many. It would be for most of us! Elijah had had enough. He was tired, he was frightened and he didn't want to be brave any longer. He went into hiding and told God that he didn't even want to live anymore.

Bekah says...

Up until this point, Elijah has just seemed like a bit of a superhero, talking to God, marching into the King's palace, having a showdown with the prophets of Baal, raising a little boy from the dead. He seemed invincible, but he was just an ordinary person like you or me, and he was having a really bad day. A super bad day, actually – worse than any bad day I've ever had!

I love that even the superheroes in the Bible were normal people like the rest of us. It gives me hope that on my bad days, on the days when I feel tired, frightened and not very brave, I'm not alone; I'm in good company.

Something to talk about

· Have you ever felt really fed up with a situation?
· What helped you get through?

Pray

Dear Lord Jesus, I'm so glad I'm not the only one to have bad days. Thank You for giving us stories like this that help us to know that other people understand how we feel. Amen.

A nap, a snack and a stroll

1 Kings 19:5–9

'Suddenly an angel touched him and said, "Wake up and eat." He looked round, and saw a loaf of bread and a jar of water near his head. He ate and drank, and lay down again. The LORD'S angel returned and woke him up a second time, saying, "Get up and eat, or the journey will be too much for you." Elijah got up, ate and drank, and the food gave him enough strength to walk forty days to Sinai, the holy mountain. There he went into a cave to spend the night.'

Something to think about

What do you imagine God might have to say to Elijah for being in such a bad mood after all He's done for him? I might expect Him to be a bit cross that Elijah had given up, or maybe He would tell Elijah to pull his socks up and get on with it, or to have more faith. But God didn't say any of that. Instead, He sent an angel to give Elijah something to eat and drink, then he suggested he had another snooze, some more food and then told him to go for a long walk. He didn't say anything else at all. Just have a snack, have a nap and take a stroll. God's brilliant.

Bekah says...

When I'm tired, I don't cope with the world very well: I get grumpy and stressed. One of the things I've learned as I've got older is that I really need to make sure I get enough sleep so that I can enjoy everything else.

Steve's amazing fact

Having a short nap is really good for you. Warmer countries like Greece, Brazil and Mexico actually have siestas. These are times in the afternoon for people to go home for a nap. In countries like these, it's said that up to 72% of people will nap up to four times per week.

Something to talk about

· What are you like when you're tired and hungry?
· What makes you feel better when you're feeling fed up?

Pray

Father God, thank You for understanding what we need better than we do. Help us to remember to rest and look after each other the way you looked after Elijah. Amen.

A still voice

1 Kings 19:9–13

'Suddenly the LORD spoke to him, "Elijah, what are you doing here?"

He answered, "LORD God Almighty... the people of Israel have broken their covenant with you... and they are trying to kill me!"

"Go out and stand before me on top of the mountain," the LORD said to him. Then the LORD passed by and sent a furious wind that split the hills and shattered the rocks — but the LORD was not in the wind. The wind stopped blowing, and then there was an earthquake — but the LORD was not in the earthquake. After the earthquake there was a fire — but the LORD was not in the fire. And after the fire there was the soft whisper of a voice.

When Elijah heard it, he covered his face with his cloak and went out and stood at the entrance of the cave.'

Something to think about

After the snack, the nap and the really rather long walk, God gives Elijah a chance to talk. God would already have known what Elijah was thinking but He also knew it was good for him to say it out loud – the last part of feeling better. Then God reminded Elijah who He was with a mighty wind, earthquake and fire, but finally in the stillness Elijah found God.

Bekah says...

I'm not very good at being still and quiet; I'm a busy, talkative kind of person. But I've learned that sometimes I just need to be still and quiet to find God. It's hard to turn off the noise of our lives sometimes, but it's important we do.

Steve says...

Extra noise in my life comes from email, WhatsApp, Facebook, Messenger, Twitter, phone calls, text messages and watching TV. It may well be the same for you. How about deciding to check on some things (like Facebook, Twitter and Instagram) just once a day? Other things, like email, you could check twice or three times a day if needed. But set a limit - you'll filter out a lot of noise.

Something to talk about

· Why don't you tell each other about what is making you sad or mad at the moment?
· Take some time to be still and ask God to help you remember Him.

Pray

Dear Lord Jesus, I choose to wait quietly with You and remember how much You love me, even when my life seems difficult. Amen.

Return

1 Kings 19:13–16

'A voice said to him, "Elijah, what are you doing here?"

He answered, "LORD God Almighty, I have always served you — you alone. But the people of Israel have broken their covenant with you, torn down your altars, and killed all your prophets. I am the only one left — and they are trying to kill me."

The LORD said, "Return to the wilderness near Damascus, then enter the city and anoint Hazael as king of Syria; anoint Jehu son of Nimshi as king of Israel, and anoint Elisha son of Shaphat from Abel Meholah to succeed you as prophet.'

Something to think about

After reminding Elijah who He was, God asks him again what's going on and listens to the answer, but this time He responds to Elijah in a new way. It's time now for Elijah to let the hurts go; it's time to think about something new, to go home and get on with his job of serving God. When hard times come, it's really easy to think about nothing else, but once we've rested and let God restore us, we need to get on with our lives – whether that's school, work or building good relationships with friends and family. It's a bit like Simba in Disney's *The Lion King*; Simba ran away to save his life, but eventually it was time to return home and become king.

Bekah says...

I once had a boss who picked on me and made up stories about me. I didn't have a clue what to do and thought about leaving my job, but I didn't. I prayed about it and then went back to work and spoke to my boss' boss, who helped me sort the situation out.

Something to talk about

· Is there a situation (like a broken friendship) that you've been avoiding?
· Is it time to try and rebuild relationships?

Pray

Dear God, thank You that You give us time to get over the things that hurt us, but that You always have a new chapter waiting for us. Amen.

Something for the weekend

Why not watch *The Lion King* together? It's not a Bible story but it's a similar story of someone running away and then being ready to return – and it's just a great film!

Hard lesson

Daniel 1:1–2

'In the third year that Jehoiakim was king of Judah, King Nebuchadnezzar of Babylonia attacked Jerusalem and surrounded the city. The Lord let him capture King Jehoiakim and seize some of the temple treasures. He took some prisoners back with him to the temple of his gods in Babylon, and put the captured treasures in the temple storerooms.'

Something to think about

God's people, the Israelites, had turned away from Him again and again and again! They'd had one bad king after another. God had given them awesome prophets, performed amazing miracles and rescued them from their enemies. God had told them that He loved them, that He wanted the best for them, and He had warned them that they were heading down a road to destruction. They just didn't listen, or if they did, they soon stopped. Eventually, God used the hardest lesson to remind the Israelites to follow Him: He allowed the king of Babylon, King Nebuchadnezzar, to win in battle against the people of Judah. He captured hundreds and thousands of God's people, and marched them and their treasures out of their Promised Land to live in a foreign land.

Bekah says...

This seems terribly harsh. But actually, I can understand how it came to happen. I can remember, as a little girl, ignoring my parents when they asked me nicely not to do something, or being good for five minutes until I thought they weren't looking. In fact, my mum loves to tell the story of me playing with her favourite dinner plates on the sideboard and saying, 'It's no good, Mummy. You're going to have to get really cross to make me stop!'

Steve's amazing fact

The Hanging Gardens of Babylon are one of the Seven Wonders of the Ancient World – but historians aren't entirely sure that they ever existed! According to legend, King Nebuchadnezzar built these beautiful gardens for his wife, Queen Amytis, because she missed the green hills and valleys of her homeland. They are called Hanging Gardens because they were built on stone terraces, high up above the ground.

Something to talk about

· What good advice have you ignored?
· What encourages you to do the right thing?

Pray

Father God, thank You for always wanting the best for us. Help us to trust You and to always follow You. Amen.

A new start

Daniel 1:3–7

'The king ordered Ashpenaz, his chief official, to select from among the Israelite exiles some young men of the royal family and of the noble families. They had to be handsome, intelligent, well-trained, quick to learn, and free from physical defects, so that they would be qualified to serve in the royal court. Ashpenaz was to teach them to read and write the Babylonian language. The king also gave orders that every day they were to be given the same food and wine as the members of the royal court. After three years of this training they were to appear before the king. Among those chosen were Daniel, Hananiah, Mishael, and Azariah, all of whom were from the tribe of Judah. The chief official gave them new names: Belteshazzar, Shadrach, Meshach, and Abednego.'

Something to think about

If you were one of those people who had been taken from your home and marched to another land, it might have been easy to think it was the end of the world. But for those four men, it was a second chance in a whole new world. They'd been chosen to serve the king. They had gifts and talents, and they could still use them, even if it wasn't in the way that they had imagined.

Steve says...

Moving house, school or job can be frightening, and having a friendship end is really sad, especially if those things aren't our choice. It can feel like the end of the world. But it's important to remember that God always has another chapter in His story for our lives and we should look out for opportunities to use our gifts and talents. Even if it's different to the way we had imagined.

Bekah says...

When my first marriage came to an end, I was devastated. I felt like all my dreams were broken. But, over time, God gave me new dreams and I've discovered this unexpected world I'm in now is more wonderful than I could have imagined.

Something to talk about

· For younger readers: What do you imagine will happen in your life in the future?
· For older readers: Does your life look very different to the way you'd imagined? How?

Pray

Father God, when life doesn't turn out the way we expect, help us to remember that You are the God of second chances and that there are still great things we can do. Amen.

New but the same

Daniel 1:8–13

'Daniel made up his mind not to let himself become ritually unclean by eating the food and drinking the wine of the royal court, so he asked Ashpenaz to help him, and God made Ashpenaz sympathetic to Daniel. Ashpenaz, however, was afraid of the king, so he said to Daniel, "The king has decided what you are to eat and drink, and if you don't look as fit as the other young men, he may kill me."

So Daniel went to the guard whom Ashpenaz had placed in charge of him and his three friends. "Test us for ten days," he said. "Give us vegetables to eat and water to drink. Then compare us with the young men who are eating the food of the royal court, and base your decision on how we look."'

Something to think about

This new start for Daniel and his friends was great, but there was a problem. The king wanted them to eat food that God had told His people not to eat. The guys had a big decision to make – should they eat the food and keep the king happy? Or should they stay faithful to God and refuse the fancy food, even though He had allowed them to be captured? What a choice! It was like being caught between the frying pan and the fire. It would have been tempting to forget God, but Daniel didn't. Despite everything that happened, Daniel remembered who God is and wanted to stay true to Him – pretty impressive.

Bekah says...

God doesn't give us rules about what we eat anymore, but that doesn't mean we don't have difficult choices to make. Sometimes we want people to think we're cool and just like them, but that might mean joining in conversations that aren't nice or doing things that aren't kind or right. It's good to think ahead about what we do and don't want to do, so that when the time comes it's easier to make the best decision.

Something to talk about

· What things wouldn't you do even if your friends were doing them?
· What would you do or say if you felt pressured to do something in order to fit in with the crowd?

Pray

God, I really want people to like me and sometimes that makes me think about doing things that aren't right or pleasing to You. I'm sorry for when I get that wrong. Amen.

A test

Daniel 1:14–20

'He agreed to let them try it for ten days. When the time was up, they looked healthier and stronger than all those who had been eating the royal food. So from then on the guard let them continue to eat vegetables instead of what the king provided.

God gave the four young men knowledge and skill in literature and philosophy. In addition, he gave Daniel skill in interpreting visions and dreams.

At the end of the three years set by the king, Ashpenaz took all the young men to Nebuchadnezzar. The king talked with them all, and Daniel, Hananiah, Mishael, and Azariah impressed him more than any of the others. So they became members of the king's court. No matter what question the king asked or what problem he raised, these four knew ten times more than any fortune teller or magician in his whole kingdom.'

Something to think about

God's people might have been far from home, but God hadn't left them. He was still watching over these guys, making sure that the king's guard saw they were fit and healthy, and helping them to be brilliant at all the tasks they were given. God helped them to stand out against all the other people who worked in the palace.

Bekah says...

I think we sometimes expect God's gifts to be something a bit supernatural, and Daniel did get an amazing gift to interpret dreams - a bit like Joseph. But for the other three, it was knowledge about literature and philosophy. It might not seem very exciting, but actually God cares about your school work and all the other ordinary things you do.

Steve's amazing fact

Did you know certain foods can help you to focus more, have a better memory, be less stressed and less tired? A recent study found that eating blueberries and strawberries could help people who have trouble remembering, learning new things, concentrating or making decisions that affect their everyday life.

Something to talk about

· What are the different places that you usually go to every week?
· How can you use the gifts God has given you in those places?

Pray

Father God, thank You for the gifts You have given me. I want to work hard for You wherever I am, so people can see how great You are. Amen.

Nightmare

Daniel 2:1–6,10

'Nebuchadnezzar... had a dream. It worried him so much that he couldn't sleep, so he sent for his fortune tellers, magicians, sorcerers, and wizards to come and explain the dream to him... he said to them, "I'm worried about a dream I have had. I want to know what it means."

They answered the king... "May Your Majesty live forever! Tell us your dream, and we will explain it to you."

The king said to them, "I have made up my mind that you must tell me the dream and then tell me what it means. If you can't, I'll have you torn limb from limb and make your houses a pile of ruins. But if you can tell me both the dream and its meaning, I will reward you with gifts and great honour."...

The advisers replied, "There is no one on the face of the earth who can tell Your Majesty what you want to know. No king, not even the greatest and most powerful, has ever made such a demand of his fortune tellers, magicians, and wizards. What Your Majesty is asking for is so difficult that no one can do it for you except the gods, and they do not live among human beings."'

Something to think about

Nebuchadnezzar was a pretty scary man. He'd totally ransacked Israel and now he was threatening to do some pretty nasty stuff to anyone who couldn't tell him what his dream meant. On top of that, he wouldn't even tell them what the dream was in the first place! How glad are you that you weren't one of his advisors? Talk about a bad boss. Remember that gift God gave Daniel though? Maybe God was putting a plan together that nobody else could see.

Steve's amazing fact

Everybody dreams. Fortunately, our bodies are created to make sure that whatever is happening in our dreamland stays there. Most of our muscles relax when we're asleep and that usually stops us from acting out our dreams. Good job!

Something to talk about

- Have there been times when you have felt scared of someone?
- How did you cope with that?

Pray

Father God, there are some scary people in the world. Please help me to remember that You are always with me. Amen.

Trick question

Daniel 2:12–19, 26

'At that, the king flew into a rage and ordered the execution of all the royal advisers in Babylon. So the order was issued for all of them to be killed, including Daniel and his friends.

Then Daniel went to Arioch, commander of the king's bodyguard, who had been ordered to carry out the execution. Choosing his words carefully, he asked Arioch why the king had issued such a harsh order. So Arioch told Daniel what had happened.

Daniel went at once and obtained royal permission for more time, so that he could tell the king what the dream meant. Then Daniel went home and told his friends Hananiah, Mishael, and Azariah what had happened. He told them to pray to the God of heaven for mercy and to ask him to explain the mystery to them so that they would not be killed along with the other advisers in Babylon.

Then that same night the mystery was revealed to Daniel in a vision, and he praised the God of heaven...

The king said to Daniel (who was also called Belteshazzar), "Can you tell me what I dreamed and what it means?"'

Something to think about

The king got very wound up by the advisors' reply and became even scarier. Daniel and his friends were in deep trouble, even though they hadn't done anything. But God was definitely at work behind the scenes. Daniel's response was amazing. He didn't panic, get angry and shout about how unfair everything was; he just quietly asked what was going on, asked for some time and then did the only thing he knew to do – he gave his worries to God. God was the only one who could help him.

Something to talk about

• Do you have a scary situation that worries you?
• Why not take some time to pray about it now?

Pray

Father God, thank You for being bigger than anything that frightens me. Help me to trust that You will look after me. Amen.

Something for the weekend

1 Peter 5:7 says, 'Leave all your worries with him, because he cares for you.' It's a great verse that reminds us that God will take care of our worries. Why not take some time to memorise this verse, or create a poster out of the words so you can remember it when you need it?

Interpretation

Daniel 2:27–30,45,47–48

'Daniel replied, "Your Majesty... there is a God in heaven, who reveals mysteries. He has informed Your Majesty what will happen in the future. Now I will tell you the dream, the vision you had while you were asleep.

"While Your Majesty was sleeping, you dreamed about the future; and God, who reveals mysteries, showed you what is going to happen. Now, this mystery was revealed to me, not because I am wiser than anyone else, but so that Your Majesty may learn the meaning of your dream and understand the thoughts that have come to you... The great God is telling Your Majesty what will happen in the future. I have told you exactly what you dreamt, and have given you its true meaning." ... The king said, "Your God is the greatest of all gods, the Lord over kings, and the one who reveals mysteries. I know this because you have been able to explain this mystery." Then he gave Daniel a high position'

Something to think about

If you read the rest of the chapter in your Bible, you can find out what the dream actually was and what it meant, but the most important thing was that Daniel didn't just use this gift God gave him to save his skin, he used it to show the king how awesome God was. Daniel didn't take the credit for knowing the dream and its meaning, and so the king recognised it as God's power. Who would have thought the mighty, scary king of Babylon would believe in God?

Steve's amazing fact

Who Moved The Stone?* is a book that looks at the evidence for the resurrection of Jesus. Convinced that the story wasn't true, the author, Frank Morison, started to write about Jesus' last days to disprove the resurrection. However, as he studied the evidence, he realised it was true and he later became a Christian.

Something to talk about

- Is there someone you know who you think would never believe in God?
- Why not pray for an opportunity for them to see how awesome God is?

Pray

Dear God, sometimes I think _____ would never follow You. Help me to remember that nothing is impossible with You, and please help them to see how awesome You are. Amen.

*Frank Morison, *Who Moved the Stone?* (London: Faber and Faber, 1930)

Change of heart

Daniel 3:1–6

'King Nebuchadnezzar had a gold statue made, 27 metres high and nearly three metres wide, and he had it set up in the plain of Dura in the province of Babylon. Then the king gave orders for all his officials to come together... They were to attend the dedication of the statue which King Nebuchadnezzar had set up. When all these officials gathered for the dedication and stood in front of the statue, a herald announced in a loud voice, "People of all nations, races, and languages! You will hear the sound of the trumpets, followed by the playing of oboes, lyres, zithers, and harps; and then all the other instruments will join in. As soon as the music starts, you are to bow down and worship the gold statue that King Nebuchadnezzar has set up. Anyone who does not bow down and worship will immediately be thrown into a blazing furnace."'

Something to think about

Old King Neb wanted everyone to know how powerful and important he was. (He didn't remember God for long.) He had an enormous statue made and ordered everyone to bow to it as though he was God. He wanted people to worship him whether they liked it or not, and had gone back to his scary ways of threatening anyone who didn't want to.

Bekah says...

It's nice when people notice something good about us, isn't it? I love it when people tell me that I've done something well, but I don't want to end up like Nebuchadnezzar - thinking I'm amazing and wanting everyone to agree. God wants us to be more like Daniel, doing the right thing and letting God take the credit.

Steve's amazing fact

At 27 metres tall, Nebuchadnezzar's statue was a pretty impressive structure. However, the world's tallest statue, unveiled in India in 2018, is of independence leader Sardar Vallabhbhai Patel and is 182 metres tall! It is nearly double the height of New York's Statue of Liberty and over four times bigger than Christ the Redeemer in Brazil. That's seriously tall!

Something to talk about

· What have you done that you're really proud of?
· How would you feel if no one knew about your achievement?

Pray

Almighty God, You are the King of kings and the Lord of lords. Help me to remember that on the days when I feel like I'm the king of the world. Amen.

Even if

Daniel 3:8–13,16–18

'It was then that some Babylonians took the opportunity to denounce the Jews. They said to King Nebuchadnezzar, "May Your Majesty live forever! Your Majesty has issued an order that as soon as the music starts, everyone is to bow down and worship the gold statue, and that anyone who does not bow down and worship it is to be thrown into a blazing furnace. There are some Jews whom you put in charge of the province of Babylon — Shadrach, Meshach, and Abednego — who are disobeying Your Majesty's orders. They do not worship your god or bow down to the statue you set up."

At that, the king flew into a rage and ordered the three men to be brought before him...

"Your Majesty, we will not try to defend ourselves. If the God whom we serve is able to save us from the blazing furnace and from your power, then he will. But even if he doesn't, Your Majesty may be sure that we will not worship your god, and we will not bow down to the gold statue that you have set up."'

Something to think about

Some of the Babylonians weren't happy that the Jews (God's people) were getting so popular with the king. They knew that Shadrach, Meshach and Abednego wouldn't bow to anything that wasn't God, so they grabbed this chance to get them into serious – and very hot – trouble. But these boys had the most amazing faith. They absolutely knew who God was, and not even a super-hot fire would persuade them to bow to the statue.

Bekah says...

The young men knew God could save them, but what really amazes me is that they said 'even if he doesn't... we will not bow down'. Their loyalty to God didn't depend on Him doing miracles for them. He's worth our loyalty whatever happens.

Steve's amazing fact

Gold has been used by people all over the world for thousands of years. It's used for things like money, decoration and jewellery, and even things like tooth repairs and electronics!

Something to talk about
· Who are you loyal to?
· Why?

Pray
Father God, thank You for always being there for us. Help us to always be loyal to You too. Amen.

Rescue

Daniel 3:19–25

'Then Nebuchadnezzar lost his temper, and his face turned red with anger at Shadrach, Meshach, and Abednego. So he ordered the furnace to be heated seven times hotter than usual. And he commanded the strongest men in his army to tie the three men up and throw them into the blazing furnace. So they tied them up, fully dressed — shirts, robes, caps, and all — and threw them into the blazing furnace. Now because the king had given strict orders for the furnace to be made extremely hot, the flames burned up the guards who took the men to the furnace. Then Shadrach, Meshach, and Abednego, still tied up, fell into the heart of the blazing fire.

Suddenly Nebuchadnezzar leaped to his feet in amazement. He asked his officials, "Didn't we tie up three men and throw them into the blazing furnace?"

They answered, "Yes, we did, Your Majesty."

"Then why do I see four men walking around in the fire?" he asked. "They are not tied up, and they show no sign of being hurt — and the fourth one looks like an angel."'

Something to think about

This is an incredible part of the story. Nebuchadnezzar had totally lost his temper and had these three amazing and brave men thrown into the fire for not worshipping him. The guards died because of the heat at the entrance, but Shadrach, Meshach and Abednego walked around in the fire and then, suddenly, it looked like someone else was there too! It might have been an angel sent to protect them, or some people even think it could have been Jesus Himself. Whoever it was, God was showing He was just as loyal as the men in the fire and that He could protect them from anything.

Steve says...

In Isaiah 43:2, God tells His people, 'When you pass through fire, you will not be burnt; the hard trials that come will not hurt you.' He sent this message through His prophet Isaiah while the Israelites were living in Babylon – that probably gave real confidence to Shadrach, Meshach and Abednego.

Something to talk about

· Do you need to know that God is with you in a particular situation?
· What helps you to remember that you're not alone?

Pray

Father God, thank You for always being with us, even when times are tough. Amen.

Jealousy

Daniel 6:7–10

'"Your Majesty should issue an order and enforce it strictly. Give orders that for thirty days no one be permitted to request anything from any god or from any human being except from Your Majesty. Anyone who violates this order is to be thrown into a pit filled with lions. So let Your Majesty issue this order and sign it, and it will be in force, a law of the Medes and Persians, which cannot be changed." And so King Darius signed the order. When Daniel learnt that the order had been signed, he went home. In an upstairs room of his house there were windows that faced toward Jerusalem. There, just as he had always done, he knelt down at the open windows and prayed to God three times a day.'

Something to think about

Daniel's friends were rescued from the fire, and King Nebuchadnezzar worshipped God again and said everyone else in the country should too. But some years later, there was a new king who didn't follow God. The court officials were still jealous of the powerful position Daniel had been given and hatched a new plan to get rid of him and his friends. This time they persuaded the king to ban people from praying to anyone but him. Sound familiar?

Bekah says...

Jealousy is a really horrible thing. It makes us want things other people have and we can end up resenting people if they have things we don't. If we let it run away with us, we can end up being unkind and hoping other people will suffer – a bit like the court officials were with Daniel and his friends.

Steve says...

I once heard of a man who divorced his wife after discovering a picture on social media of her kissing a horse. The woman said she had posted the photo of her equine smooch herself. That's some serious jealousy going on there.

Something to talk about

· Have you ever been jealous of someone?
· How did that affect your relationship?

Pray

Father God, help me to be pleased for other people when they have nice things or do things I'd like to do. Please help me to let go of jealousy before it controls me. Amen.

Turnaround

Daniel 6:11–12,16–22

'When Daniel's enemies observed him praying to God, all of them went together to the king to accuse Daniel. They said, "Your Majesty, you signed an order that for the next thirty days anyone who requested anything from any god or from any human being except you, would be thrown into a pit filled with lions."

... So the king gave orders for Daniel to be arrested and he was thrown into the pit filled with lions. He said to Daniel, "May your God, whom you serve so loyally, rescue you." A stone was put over the mouth of the pit... so that no one could rescue Daniel. Then the king returned to the palace and spent a sleepless night, without food or any form of entertainment.

At dawn the king got up and hurried to the pit. When he got there, he called out anxiously, "Daniel, servant of the living God! Was the God you serve so loyally able to save you from the lions?"

Daniel answered, "May Your Majesty live forever! God sent his angel to shut the mouths of the lions so that they would not hurt me."'

Something to think about

Just like before, God rescued Daniel. God has an amazing ability to turn terrible situations into good ones. He took the king's bad decision, the officials' jealousy and the hungry lions, and used them as a recipe to show His power. Once again the king of Babylon was reminded that no matter how powerful a king he was, God was mightier. Once again the king bowed down and worshipped God, and told the rest of the country to do the same. Nothing is impossible for God.

Something to talk about

· Do you need God to turn around a situation in your life?
· What would you like to see Him do?

Pray

Father God, You are amazing at turning situations around. Nothing is impossible for You. Thank You. Amen.

Something for the weekend

Daniel and his friends were really good at doing the right thing, even if no one noticed or it got them into trouble. Why not put everyone's names in a hat, take it in turns to pull out a name, and then be kind and generous to that person all weekend? You could even try doing it secretly.

Word

John 1:1–9

'In the beginning the Word already existed; the Word was with God, and the Word was God. From the very beginning the Word was with God. Through him God made all things; not one thing in all creation was made without him. The Word was the source of life, and this life brought light to humanity. The light shines in the darkness, and the darkness has never put it out.

God sent his messenger, a man named John, who came to tell people about the light, so that all should hear the message and believe. He himself was not the light; he came to tell about the light. This was the real light – the light that comes into the world and shines on everyone.'

Something to think about

Over the next few weeks, we're going to look at what happened when people met Jesus for real, when He walked around on earth as a human. The events are told by one of Jesus' best friends: a man called John. He starts this book of stories about Jesus with this slightly complicated explanation of who he'd realised that Jesus was – he calls Him the Word, the Son of God, with God and part of God. He explains that Jesus might have been born as a man that first Christmas but He'd existed before. He made the world and everything in it, and He still gives people life and brings light into the darkness.

Just to confuse things, John introduces another John in

verse 6. This John is Jesus' cousin, sometimes called John the Baptist, who God gave the job of telling people that Jesus was coming. More about him tomorrow!

Steve's amazing fact

Apart from Jesus, John the Baptist is probably one of the most significant figures in the Gospels. Like Jesus, his birth was well documented (Luke 1:5–25). His entrance into the world was marked by angelic proclamation and amazing divine intervention (Luke 1:57–80). John's birth has lots of parallels with that of Jesus, so John is clearly a key figure in the gospel story.

Something to talk about

· How would you explain who Jesus is?
· Why is He special to you?

Pray

Dear Lord Jesus, You were there before the world began, before everything. You created me. You're amazing! Amen.

Not a hero

John 1:19–23

'The Jewish authorities in Jerusalem sent some priests and Levites to John, to ask him, "Who are you?"

John did not refuse to answer, but spoke out openly and clearly, saying: "I am not the Messiah."

"Who are you, then?" they asked. "Are you Elijah?"

"No, I am not," John answered.

"Are you the Prophet?" they asked.

"No," he replied.

"Then tell us who you are," they said. "We have to take an answer back to those who sent us. What do you say about yourself?"

John answered by quoting the prophet Isaiah: "I am 'the voice of someone shouting in the desert: Make a straight path for the Lord to travel!'"'

Something to think about

John the Baptist did what his name said: he baptised people in the River Jordan. Normally people who changed religion to become Jews got baptised to symbolise that they were starting afresh and washing away their old lives. But John was baptising people who were already Jews, which made the Jewish leaders wonder who he was, with his weird ways.

God's people, the Jews, were waiting for a saviour to

come and rescue them from the Romans. They even wondered if one of the old heroes like Moses or Elijah might come back from the dead to do it! John was quick to tell everyone, 'Don't look at me, I'm not the hero. I'm just here to point Him out to you.'

Bekah says...

Years ago, my car broke down while I was driving somewhere with my two little girls. We had to wait a couple of hours in the dark for the RAC to come. They towed the car and the three of us sat with the driver in the front of the truck. Gem and Meg kept calling the man 'our hero'. I'm sure it made his day.

Steve says...

John had a very simple lifestyle. He certainly wasn't a man who enjoyed or needed his home comforts. He lived in the wilderness, wore camel hair clothes, and might have done well on *I'm a Celebrity... Get Me Out of Here!* as his diet seemed to consist of surviving on locusts and wild honey.

Something to talk about

· Have you ever needed rescuing?
· Did you have to wait long?

Pray

Jesus, thank You for being the very best hero – the one who never lets us down. Amen.

The hero

John 1:29–34

'The next day John saw Jesus coming to him, and said, "There is the Lamb of God, who takes away the sin of the world! This is the one I was talking about when I said, 'A man is coming after me, but he is greater than I am, because he existed before I was born.' I did not know who he would be, but I came baptizing with water in order to make him known to the people of Israel."

And John gave this testimony: "I saw the Spirit come down like a dove from heaven and stay on him. I still did not know that he was the one, but God, who sent me to baptize with water, had said to me, 'You will see the Spirit come down and stay on a man; he is the one who baptizes with the Holy Spirit.' I have seen it," said John, "and I tell you that he is the Son of God."'

Something to think about

John had grown up with Jesus – he was a few months older than Him – but it was only recently that John had realised that Jesus was no ordinary cousin. He told everyone that he had seen God's Spirit come down and stay on Jesus, and that this was the sign He was the Son of God.

In the past, God's Spirit had come down on people for a short while to give them superhuman strength like Samson or to prophesy like Elijah. But God's Spirit stayed with Jesus because He was God too. That meant He could give the Spirit to others so that they could have God with them all the time and have the power to follow Him well.

Steve's amazing fact

Doves are often used as symbols of peace and love or as messengers throughout the Bible. This started in Genesis when God flooded the earth and a dove indicated to Noah that the waters were receding and there was dry land, but it is also shown in the New Testament Gospels describing the baptism of Jesus.

Something to talk about

· When did you first realise who Jesus is?
· What helped you to find out?

Pray

Jesus, You are the Son of God. Please fill me with Your Spirit so that I will always have You with me. Amen.

Time with Jesus

John 1:35–39

'The next day John was standing there again with two of his disciples, when he saw Jesus walking by. "There is the Lamb of God!" he said.

The two disciples heard him say this and went with Jesus. Jesus turned, saw them following him, and asked, "What are you looking for?"

They answered, "Where do you live, Rabbi?" (This word means "Teacher.")

"Come and see," he answered. (It was then about four o'clock in the afternoon.) So they went with him and saw where he lived, and spent the rest of that day with him.'

Something to think about

John had lots of followers but he wasn't greedy or big-headed about it. He didn't want to be the centre of attention – he wanted Jesus to be. When Jesus came along, John pointed Him out so that his followers could follow Jesus instead. John always knew his job was to point to someone way more important than him and then to step back out of the way. That's pretty humble.

Bekah says...

I love that even though Jesus was the Son of God and knew everything, He still asks the men what they want to do, so that they have a choice. God never makes us do anything. These two disciples make the best choice – they go to spend time with Jesus and find out more about Him. It changes their lives forever and they follow Him for the rest of their lives. Spending time with Jesus is always a good choice.

Steve's amazing fact

In a recent poll, David Attenborough and the Queen were voted the British public's most admired people. In a magazine interview, I was recently asked which famous people I'd most like to have over for a meal. Stephen Fry, Peter Kay and Kylie Minogue would be my perfect dinner guests. I wonder who'd be on your list.

Something to talk about

- If you could have an afternoon with Jesus like the two disciples did, what would you like to do?
- What would you want to talk about?

Pray

Jesus, thank You for asking if I'd like to follow You. I choose to spend time with You – I want to know You more. Amen.

A new name

John 1:39–42

'So they went with him and saw where he lived, and spent the rest of that day with him.

One of them was Andrew, Simon Peter's brother. At once he found his brother Simon and told him, "We have found the Messiah." (This word means "Christ.") Then he took Simon to Jesus.

Jesus looked at him and said, "Your name is Simon son of John, but you will be called Cephas." (This is the same as Peter and means "a rock.")'

Something to think about

Andrew had spent the afternoon with Jesus and it had blown his mind. He didn't want to keep his new friend to himself; he was desperate to tell people about Him. First, he went to the most important person in his life, his brother Simon.

Everyone who meets Jesus has their own unique experience. Simon certainly did. Jesus gave him a nickname that became a whole new identity for him. Cephas wasn't even a proper name – it was more like Jesus took one look at Simon and said, 'I'm going to call you Rocky.' What a cool nickname. Simon wouldn't know for years that this was

Jesus showing that one day he would be a tough, strong guy who would travel the world telling people about Him and coping with some really difficult times along the way.

Steve's amazing fact

As a young man, Charles de Gaulle, who went on to become a famous French general and president, was given the nickname 'The Big Asparagus'. It was a pretty harsh insult and was given to him by his fellow cadets in the military academy – they found his tall height rather funny.

Something to talk about

· Have you ever had a nickname?
· If you could use one word to describe each other, what would it be?

Pray

Father God, thank You for knowing me inside and out. Please show me what You call me – the names You've given me. Amen.

Amazing

John 1:43–49

'The next day Jesus decided to go to Galilee. He found Philip and said to him, "Come with me!" (Philip was from Bethsaida, the town where Andrew and Peter lived.) Philip found Nathanael and told him, "We have found the one whom Moses wrote about in the book of the Law and whom the prophets also wrote about. He is Jesus son of Joseph, from Nazareth."

"Can anything good come from Nazareth?" Nathanael asked.

"Come and see," answered Philip.

When Jesus saw Nathanael coming to him, he said about him, "Here is a real Israelite; there is nothing false in him!"

Nathanael asked him, "How do you know me?"

Jesus answered, "I saw you when you were under the fig tree before Philip called you."

"Teacher," answered Nathanael, "you are the Son of God! You are the King of Israel!"'

Something to think about

More and more people were seeing Jesus, and it seems that anyone who spent much time with Him wanted their friends to know Him too. Philip was just the same. Straight away he realised that Jesus was pretty special, that He might even be the hero everyone had been waiting for. He went to tell his friend Nathanael, who wasn't so sure. Philip didn't spend ages trying to prove who Jesus was, but just invited his friend to see for himself. He left the rest up to Jesus and Nathanael, and he wasn't disappointed: Jesus blew Nathanael away by knowing who he was without him having to say anything.

Steve says...

Telling our friends about Jesus can seem impossible, but maybe we could just invite them to come and see like Philip and Andrew did. People often have lots of questions and it can feel too hard to answer them all, but the good news is that we don't need to – we just need to invite them to come and see Jesus for themselves.

Pray

Lord Jesus, thank You that You never disappoint. Help me to invite people to come and see You too. Amen.

Something for the weekend

Create a list of people you'd love to know Jesus. Could you invite them to come and see for themselves who Jesus is – at a club at church, or a special service or event? If there's nothing on right now perhaps you could plan a special event yourselves.

Not the right time

John 2:1–5

'Two days later there was a wedding in the town of Cana in Galilee. Jesus' mother was there, and Jesus and his disciples had also been invited to the wedding. When the wine had given out, Jesus' mother said to him, "They are out of wine."

"You must not tell me what to do," Jesus replied. "My time has not yet come."

Jesus' mother then told the servants, "Do whatever he tells you."'

Something to think about

Back when Jesus walked on earth as a human, all kinds of leaders had disciples. These were particular kinds of friends – people who wanted to learn from them and be like them and who went with them everywhere. Jesus and His friends went to a wedding where they met His mum too, but then there was a disaster: the wine ran out. That might not sound like a disaster to you, but it would have been a huge embarrassment to the wedding family. It was like running out of turkey at Christmas! Mary knew her boy Jesus could fix it, but Jesus knew it was not quite time for Him to show people who He was.

Bekah says...

Waiting for God's timing is difficult sometimes. I like things to happen quickly and go my way, but God isn't always like that. Jesus told His mum to wait, so she gave the servants the best advice ever: just do what Jesus tells you. It's still good advice - while we're waiting for Jesus to solve our problems or change our situations, we can still do what He tells us. We can be kind, love one another and speak the truth.

Steve's amazing fact

A wedding in Bible times was a very special occasion – even more so than now. After the wedding ceremony itself, the wedding feast began and this huge celebration lasted a full seven days at the bridegroom's house. All guests were given special clothes, the bridegroom and bride were treated as royalty and there was lots of food, wine and dancing.

Something to talk about

· When have you had to wait a long time for God to answer your prayers?
· How did that feel?

Pray

Jesus, thank You for always listening to our prayers, even when You tell us to wait. Help us to be patient and trust You. Amen.

No shame

John 2:6–10

'The Jews have rules about ritual washing, and for this purpose six stone water jars were there, each one large enough to hold about a hundred litres. Jesus said to the servants, "Fill these jars with water." They filled them to the brim, and then he told them, "Now draw some water out and take it to the man in charge of the feast." They took him the water, which now had turned into wine, and he tasted it. He did not know where this wine had come from (but, of course, the servants who had drawn out the water knew); so he called the bridegroom and said to him, "Everyone else serves the best wine first, and after the guests have had plenty to drink, he serves the ordinary wine. But you have kept the best wine until now!"'

Something to think about

The servants waited to see what Jesus said and then filled the big jars with water. Imagine their surprise when they discovered them full of wine! They didn't tell anyone where the wine came from, maybe because Jesus wasn't ready for everyone to know He could do miracles, but they must have been blown away by what they saw. The boss was just confused. He couldn't understand why the best wine was saved till last!

Bekah says...

It's great that Jesus did this miracle on the low down. He wasn't ready to make a big show, but He didn't want the wedding family to be embarrassed either, so He just quietly fixed it and fixed it well. I don't like it when people embarrass me in public, so I love knowing that Jesus would never do that to me.

Steve says...

Our kids all have a different way of eating a cooked breakfast. Some don't want anything to touch anything else on the plate. Some eat the bacon first; some eat the beans first; another breaks the yoke of the egg so it soaks the toast, before covering it all back up with chopped up egg white. But they all like to save the best till last.

Something to talk about

· What's your most embarrassing moment?
· What would have made it better?

Pray

Father God, thank You for never wanting to embarrass us. Thank You for loving us without end. Amen.

Angry

John 2:13–17

'It was almost time for the Passover Festival, so Jesus went to Jerusalem. There in the Temple he found people selling cattle, sheep, and pigeons, and also the moneychangers sitting at their tables. So he made a whip from cords and drove all the animals out of the Temple, both the sheep and the cattle; he overturned the tables of the moneychangers and scattered their coins; and he ordered those who sold the pigeons, "Take them out of here! Stop making my Father's house a market place!" His disciples remembered that the scripture says, "My devotion to your house, O God, burns in me like a fire."'

Something to think about

This story shows a whole different side of Jesus. A very different kind of meeting. Jesus doesn't ever want to embarrass people, but that doesn't mean He'll stay quiet if people are doing something wrong.

God's Temple was meant to be a place for people to spend time with God. They would bring sacrifices to the Temple – special gifts to show their love for God and to say sorry for doing things wrong. But over time, some people had set up businesses in the Temple to make money out of people who wanted to say sorry to God. They were overcharging people and taking advantage of the poor. And that made Jesus angry. So angry that He tipped their tables over and chased them out of the building. It was bad behaviour anywhere, but especially in God's house.

Steve's amazing fact

Fair trade is a way of buying and selling products that allows the farmers to be paid a fair price for their produce and have better working conditions. The first product labelled as Fairtrade was Green and Black's Maya Gold chocolate in 1994. Since then, many more things have been given the Fairtrade label, including certain fruit, sugar, tea, coffee, chocolate, and even gold and silver!

Something to talk about

· When you buy things, do you know where they come from?
· What do you know about Fairtrade?

Pray

Dear God, help me to be like You and care about how people make their money. I want to think before I buy. Amen.

Born again

John 3:1–6

'There was a Jewish leader named Nicodemus, who belonged to the party of the Pharisees. One night he went to Jesus and said to him, "Rabbi, we know that you are a teacher sent by God. No one could perform the miracles you are doing unless God were with him."

Jesus answered, "I am telling you the truth: no one can see the Kingdom of God without being born again."

"How can a grown man be born again?" Nicodemus asked. "He certainly cannot enter his mother's womb and be born a second time!"

"I am telling you the truth," replied Jesus. "No one can enter the Kingdom of God without being born of water and the Spirit. A person is born physically of human parents, but is born spiritually of the Spirit."'

Something to think about

Nicodemus was a religious man and he could recognise that Jesus was sent from God. He wanted to be able to get to know Jesus, but Jesus told him the strangest thing – that he would have to be born again to be part of God's Kingdom (or God's family). 'Born again' is a funny phrase that you still hear people use today.

This all happened a long time ago, before modern science, but even Nicodemus knew you couldn't be born twice. So Jesus explained: it's not about getting back inside your mum. (Eww – what a thought!) It's about being born of the Spirit, asking God's Spirit to come in and give you a whole different kind of life. It's being born again into a new life with Jesus.

Steve's amazing fact
The heaviest baby ever born only lived 11 hours and was known as Babe. He weighed 22lbs and was 71cm long when he was born in 1879 in Ohio, USA. His parents were both nearly eight foot tall and met working in a sideshow. The pair were known as the tallest couple alive.

Something to talk about
• Why not ask your grown-ups about the day you were born – what was that like?
• If you haven't already, you could ask for God's Spirit to come into your life.

Pray
Dear Lord Jesus, thank You for making me and giving me life. I want to walk with You in a new life too. Amen.

Water

John 4:6–10

'Jesus, tired out by the journey, sat down by the well. It was about noon.

A Samaritan woman came to draw some water, and Jesus said to her, "Give me a drink of water." (His disciples had gone into town to buy food.)

The woman answered, "You are a Jew, and I am a Samaritan — so how can you ask me for a drink?" (Jews will not use the same cups and bowls that Samaritans use.)

Jesus answered, "If you only knew what God gives and who it is that is asking you for a drink, you would ask him, and he would give you life-giving water."'

Something to think about

We're never told the name of the lady in the story, but she had the most incredible meeting with Jesus. Incredible, mostly because it's weird that Jesus met with her at all. She lived in a country called Samaria, and no decent Jew would normally go anywhere near Samaria because they thought of them as an enemy. Not only that, but this Samaritan was a woman and Jewish men didn't think much of women either. On top of all that, she was at the well at lunch time, which means she was avoiding the other women who would have gone to the well in the cool of the morning. That was a clear sign that no one really liked her. But Jesus spoke to her anyway and gave her a clue that He was more than just a man and that He wanted to give her a gift that was better than water.

Bekah says...

We need water to physically stay alive, but Jesus was saying that He was like the water we need for that new life we talked about yesterday, and that He will keep us going forever. Pretty awesome.

Steve's amazing fact

None of us can survive without water but, sadly, over 600 million people in the world don't have access to clean water. In Nigeria, for example, it is estimated that one in three people are without clean water.

Something to talk about

· Have you ever been left out like this lady was?
· Who makes you feel included?

Pray

God, thank You that You include everyone. You never leave people out – everyone is welcome with You. Amen.

Transformed

John 4:16–20,25–26,28–9

"'Go and call your husband," Jesus told her, "and come back."

"I haven't got a husband," she answered.

Jesus replied, "You are right when you say you haven't got a husband. You have been married to five men, and the man you live with now is not really your husband. You have told me the truth."

"I see you are a prophet, sir," the woman said. "My Samaritan ancestors worshipped God on this mountain, but you Jews say that Jerusalem is the place where we should worship God."...

The woman said to him, "I know that the Messiah will come, and when he comes, he will tell us everything."

Jesus answered, "I am he, I who am talking with you."...

Then the woman left her water jar, went back to the town, and said to the people there, "Come and see the man who told me everything I have ever done. Could he be the Messiah?"'

Something to think about

Jesus had a really deep conversation with this lady. They didn't just talk about the weather; they talked about the stuff that really mattered. Jesus knew her background. He knew she'd had lots of husbands who had rejected her. He knew that people looked down at her – but He didn't. He'd taken time out to sit and talk with her, and then He told her the most amazing thing. People had started to wonder if Jesus was something special, but He hadn't actually told anyone who He really was yet. Not until he met the woman at the well. He told her before anyone else.

Bekah says...

Jesus chose this woman out of everyone in the world to be the first person to hear that He was the Messiah. What an incredible honour. And what a meeting! This lunchtime chat with Jesus changed the woman forever. She'd been hiding from the village, but after talking with Jesus she ran back to tell everyone about Him. That's an amazing transformation.

Pray

Dear Lord Jesus, thank You for revealing who You really are, and thank You that this news is for everyone. Amen.

Something for the weekend

We learned the other day that millions of people don't have access to clean water. Find out online what charities such as Water Aid and Tearfund are doing to help people get clean water.

Healed

John 4:46–53

'Then Jesus went back to Cana in Galilee... A government official was there whose son was ill in Capernaum. When he heard that Jesus had come from Judea to Galilee, he went to him and asked him to go to Capernaum and heal his son, who was about to die. Jesus said to him, "None of you will ever believe unless you see miracles and wonders."

"Sir," replied the official, "come with me before my child dies."

Jesus said to him, "Go, your son will live!"

The man believed Jesus' words and went. On his way home his servants met him with the news, "Your boy is going to live!"

He asked them what time it was when his son got better, and they answered, "It was one o'clock yesterday afternoon when the fever left him." Then the father remembered that it was at that very hour that Jesus had told him, "Your son will live." So he and all his family believed.'

Something to think about

Here's another meeting with Jesus that changed everything. Word was getting around about the amazing things He was doing, so this government official, desperate to save his son, came to ask Jesus to do something. It's interesting that

Jesus was a bit disappointed that everyone needed to see miracles to believe in Him, but He still healed the boy. At least two lives were transformed that day by Jesus.

Steve says...

It's good to think about Jesus' question: do we only believe in God if we see Him do miracles, or do we believe even when He doesn't? The truth is, we don't often see God heal people like this (although it definitely happens) and our faith needs to be based on who God is and what Jesus did for us, not on the miracles we see.

Something to talk about

· What made you believe that God is real and worth worshipping?
· Have you ever seen a miracle?

Pray

Dear Lord Jesus, thank You for Your great love for us and for Your great power. Help us to believe in You, whatever is going on in the world. Amen.

What do you want?

John 5:2–8

'Near the Sheep Gate in Jerusalem there is a pool with five porches; in Hebrew it is called Bethzatha. A large crowd of sick people were lying on the porches—the blind, the lame, and the paralysed. A man was there who had been ill for 38 years. Jesus saw him lying there, and he knew that the man had been ill for such a long time; so he asked him, "Do you want to get well?"

The sick man answered, "Sir, I have no one here to put me in the pool when the water is stirred up; while I am trying to get in, somebody else gets there first."

Jesus said to him, "Get up, pick up your mat, and walk." Immediately the man got well; he picked up his mat and started walking.'

Something to think about

Today we're introduced to another man whose life was turned around after a meeting with Jesus. He had been ill for 38 years – that is a *long* time – but it took seconds for Jesus to heal him. Jesus' power was beyond any human. He was God in a human body.

Imagine seeing this happen, and imagine having it

happen to you! How awesome. But, as the story carries on, there were people who just got grumpy about the man carrying his mat and Jesus healing people on the Sabbath. It turns out, seeing miracles doesn't always make people believe in Jesus. We get to choose our reaction.

Bekah says...

Someone once told me that we always get to choose our reaction to things – no matter how big or horrible or sad those things might be. It's tough to remember that, but actually it's quite liberating!

Steve's amazing fact

In this amazing story, the pool is said to have five porches, which paints a strange picture of it being five-sided. Some people suggested that this wasn't actually true and was added into the story. But in the late nineteenth century, archaeologists dug up the site and what did they find? A pool with five sides, each with a porch!

Something to talk about

· Is there something you would like God to change or heal?
· Why not ask Him to do that now?

Pray

Father God, You are awesome and full of power. Please transform my life, like You did for this man. Amen.

Supersizing

John 6:5–11

'Jesus looked around and saw that a large crowd was coming to him, so he asked Philip, "Where can we buy enough food to feed all these people?" (He said this to test Philip; actually he already knew what he would do.)

Philip answered, "... it would take more than 200 silver coins to buy enough bread."

Another of his disciples, Andrew... said, "There is a boy here who has five loaves of barley bread and two fish. But they will certainly not be enough for all these people."

"Make the people sit down," Jesus told them... there were about 5,000 men. Jesus took the bread, gave thanks to God, and distributed it to the people who were sitting there. He did the same with the fish, and they all had as much as they wanted.'

Something to think about

Lots of people met Jesus on this day, and the day must have been even more special for the little boy. He had his lunch box turned into enough food for thousands of people. How amazing to have a part in God's plan to look after the crowd!

It can feel like we don't have much to offer Jesus, but we need to remember that God can take our little things and turn them into enough. It's what He does – whether that's a few bread rolls and fish, or our time, talents or pennies. He's the God that supersizes what we give Him.

Bekah says...

I sometimes wonder about the boy's mum. She doesn't get a mention – maybe she had stayed at home – but she was probably the one who packed his lunch and taught him to share. As grown-ups, it's good to know that we can equip and prepare our kids to be ready for their part in Jesus' story.

Steve says...

In the story they only counted the men in the crowd, so we have to add the women and children. That makes it more like 20,000 people. The feeding of the 5,000 was probably an even greater miracle than you first thought.

Something to talk about

· How easy do you find it to share what you have?
· What gifts do you have that you could give Jesus?

Pray

Father God, help us to be as ready as the little boy was to share what we have with others. Amen.

Missed it

John 7:28–31,40–41

'As Jesus taught in the Temple, he said in a loud voice, "Do you really know me and know where I am from? I have not come on my own authority. He who sent me, however, is truthful. You do not know him, but I know him, because I come from him and he sent me."

Then they tried to seize him, but no one laid a hand on him, because his hour had not yet come. But many in the crowd believed in him and said, "When the Messiah comes, will he perform more miracles than this man has?"...

Some of the people in the crowd heard him... and said, "This man is really the Prophet!"

Others said, "He is the Messiah!"

But others said, "The Messiah will not come from Galilee!"'

Something to think about

You might think that if you saw Jesus face to face, it would make following Him easy. But this story shows it's not that simple. A whole bunch of people met Jesus in the Temple and saw Him do amazing things. Some of them worked out who He was, but others thought He didn't look like the hero they had imagined God would send and it couldn't possibly be Him, so instead of following Him they tried to take Him away and hurt Him.

Bekah says

It's easy to think we'd have recognised Jesus if we'd seen Him on earth, but maybe we wouldn't have. It's amazing how many people missed Him. I think we still do sometimes – we miss the things He does in our lives now. Sometimes it's just little things like the sun shining, or someone being kind, or a helpful message from a friend. They're all gifts from God.

Steve says...

I do love an unlikely hero. When I was eight years old I first read the brilliant book Watership Down. It's a story of ordinary little rabbits, and everything in the world is out to get them. To survive in that dark, dangerous world, they have to be so brave and brilliant that they become epic heroes in spite of their weaknesses.

Something to talk about
· If you could have any superpower, what would it be?
· Why?

Pray
Lord Jesus, thank You for coming to save the world. Help me to always recognise You and to see what You are doing in my life. Amen.

Changed

John 8:3–7,9–11

'The teachers of the Law and the Pharisees brought in a woman who had been caught committing adultery, and they made her stand before them all. "Teacher," they said to Jesus, "this woman was caught in the very act of committing adultery. In our Law Moses commanded that such a woman must be stoned to death. Now, what do you say?" They said this to trap Jesus, so that they could accuse him...

[Jesus] said to them, "Whichever one of you has committed no sin may throw the first stone at her." When they heard this, they all left, one by one, the older ones first. Jesus was left alone, with the woman still standing there... and said to her, "Where are they? Is there no one left to condemn you?"

"No one, sir," she answered.

"Well, then," Jesus said, "I do not condemn you either. Go, but do not sin again."'

Something to think about

This lady had been caught doing something she shouldn't and everyone was angry with her. The Pharisees, who didn't like Jesus, tried to trap Him – how could He be kind to this lady and still make sure that He encouraged truth and doing the right thing? She deserved a punishment, in their opinion. But they'd underestimated Jesus. He's the King of second chances, so He told this woman to go home. What a kind gift. He then asked her to change her life and not make the same mistakes again. It's like that for us – Jesus gives us a second chance, but He wants us to use it to be different and not just keep on making the same mistakes.

Steve's amazing fact

Thomas Edison, the inventor of the light bulb, was told by his teachers that he was 'too stupid to learn anything'. Work wasn't much better either – he was fired from his first two jobs. But he kept going and tried to learn from his mistakes. Edison made 1,000 unsuccessful attempts at inventing the light bulb before it finally worked.

Something to talk about

· When have you had a second chance?
· How did that feel?

Pray

Dear Lord Jesus, thank You for my second chances. Please help me to make the most of them. Amen.

Believe

John 10:23–30

'Jesus was walking in Solomon's Porch in the Temple, when the people gathered round him and asked, "How long are you going to keep us in suspense? Tell us the plain truth: are you the Messiah?"

Jesus answered, "I have already told you, but you would not believe me. The things I do by my Father's authority speak on my behalf; but you will not believe, for you are not my sheep. My sheep listen to my voice; I know them, and they follow me. I give them eternal life, and they shall never die. No one can snatch them away from me. What my Father has given me is greater than everything, and no one can snatch them away from the Father's care. The Father and I are one."'

Something to think about

This group of people always wanted more information from Jesus, but He'd already told them everything they needed to know. He'd told them who He was, but they'd chosen not to follow Him. And they were missing out. The beautiful thing is that Jesus promises that if you choose to follow Him, God will take care of you like a shepherd looks after his sheep, and nothing can ever take you away from Him. What a great promise.

Bekah says...

I decided to follow Jesus when I was just four years old, doing a Bible reading a bit like this with my mum and dad. All kinds of things have happened since then, but I have always known that my Father God in heaven holds me safe and tight, and He will never, ever let me go.

Steve says...

I became a Christian at a Boys' Brigade camp in Devon when I was a teenager. Ever since, I have loved helping other people to discover that they can make the same choice. I enjoy it so much, I've spent my life travelling the world and telling people how amazing Jesus is.

Something to talk about

· Have you decided to follow Jesus?
· How does it feel to know that if you choose to follow Him, He'll never let you go?

Pray

Dear Lord Jesus, thank You for always holding me tight. I choose to follow You and let You look after me forever. Amen.

Something for the weekend

The little boy in the story on Wednesday shared his lunch box. Could you share some food with someone – either by inviting people over or giving some food to your local food bank?

Other books to help you journey together...

Take time out each day to encounter the God who created you, loves you and has plans for each of you! Over 12 weeks discover more about what it means to follow God, as Steve and Bekah Legg bring a fun, engaging and personal approach to reading the Bible.

"A great resource to bring the family together to talk about the things that matter."
Rob Parsons

ISBN: 978-1-78951-265-9
(Available August 2020)

ISBN: 978-1-78259-999-9

ISBN: 978-1-78259-798-8

ISBN: 978-1-78259-692-9

Bekah is the Associate Pastor at Maybridge Community Church, and Steve is the founding editor of *Sorted* magazine. They are experienced parents of five daughters.

To find out more and to order,
visit **cwr.org.uk/thefamilydevotional** or call **01252 784700**.

Also available in Christian bookshops.

Connecting with God, your family and others

Waverley Abbey College

Courses and seminars

Publishing and media

Conference facilities

Transforming lives

CWR's vision is to enable people to experience personal transformation through applying God's Word to their lives and relationships.

Our Bible-based training and resources help people around the world to:
• Grow in their walk with God
• Understand and apply Scripture to their lives
• Resource themselves and their church
• Develop pastoral care and counselling skills
• Train for leadership
• Strengthen relationships, marriage and family life and much more.

CWR Applying God's Word
to everyday life and relationships

CWR, Waverley Abbey House,
Waverley Lane, Farnham,
Surrey GU9 8EP, UK

Telephone: **+44 (0)1252 784700**
Email: **info@cwr.org.uk**
Website: **www.cwr.org.uk**

Registered Charity No. 294387
Company Registration No. 1990308

Our insightful writers provide daily Bible reading notes and other resources for all ages, and our experienced course designers and presenters have gained an international reputation for excellence and effectiveness.

CWR's Training and Conference Centre in Surrey, England, provides excellent facilities in an idyllic setting – ideal for both learning and spiritual refreshment.